Trampoline Tumbling Today

Trampoline Tumbling Today

by

Larry Griswold and Glenn Wilson

SECOND REVISED EDITION

South Brunswick and New York: A. S. Barnes and Company
London: Thomas Yoseloff Ltd

Library of Congress Catalogue Card Number: 71-81672

A.S. Barnes and Co., Inc.
Cranbury, New Jersey 08512

Thomas Yoseloff Ltd
108 New Bond Street
London WlY OQX, England

REPRINT, 1975

SBN 498 07508 7
Printed in the United States of America

To that most wonderful of all gymnasts
the circus performer

"Between the ages of ten and twenty-two, I spent many hours each day on the trampoline learning new tricks and perfecting old routines. Most of the activity and good health I now enjoy I definitely attribute to the well-balanced exercises I obtained on the trampoline. It is splendid recreation for everyone."

JOE E. BROWN

Contents

Foreword

I am delighted to write a foreword to this manual on trampoline tumbling, for I think that the trampoline is one of the most interesting pieces of apparatus in the gymnasium. First, the high flight made possible by the springs makes "working" this piece of equipment a most delightful sensation—one similar to that experienced in diving from the springboard, except that it is repeated time and time again on the trampoline, and not just once every few minutes, as in diving. Second, the trampoline makes possible a much greater variety in tumbling activities than is possible on the ordinary floor mats. Landings and take-offs are possible from so many more positions on the trampoline that stunts can be executed which even an experienced tumbler would not dream of attempting on a mat. Third, because of the high bounce and the relatively long time execution of stunts which this high bounce allows, both men and women who are too old to tumble on floor mats, or who could not easily learn mat tumbling because of lack of spring, may engage in trampoline tumbling with profit and delight. I am, personally, somewhat past the time when it is fun to tumble on the mats; but I am doing stunts on the trampoline that I would not have thought of attempting when I was a mat tumbler in college. The trampoline is truly a device for the young and old of both sexes.

The trampoline is more than just another device for increasing the fun element in the gymnasium class. It is a splendid conditioner; and, in addition to this, it is one of our best pieces of apparatus for motor education. On the trampoline, one learns more about spatial adaptation, quick reactions to emergencies of balance, and fine motor timing than on any other gymnastic device with which I am acquainted.

One precaution needs to be kept in mind—that of safety. This does not mean that the trampoline is dangerous: properly used, it is not. But any piece of gymnasium apparatus is potentially dangerous if improperly used or supervised, and this applies to the trampoline. ALWAYS, even if the performer is expert, someone should stand ready *at each end* of the trampoline to "protect" in case of a bit of carelessness. Learners should never attempt to make too rapid progress, undertaking the more difficult stunts before the fundamentals have been thoroughly learned—a mistake which this manual, with its system of progressive learning, endeavors to anticipate and correct. The trampoline should never be left available for use without proper supervision, but should be folded and locked when the instructor is not at hand. If the student observes these precautions and follows the advice given in this manual, he will be able to engage with safety in one of the most delightful forms ot gymnastics in existence.

DR. C. H. McCLOY
Professor of Physical Education
State University of Iowa

Acknowledgments

In preparing the material presented in this book, we have been extremely fortunate in having had the help, cooperation, and encouragement of many persons—physical educators, professional performers, and friends from many walks of life. We wish to offer, in these few paragraphs, our sincere thanks to all those whose interest and assistance was of immeasurable value, and to acknowledge special indebtedness to the following:

George Paul and Charles Keeney, eminent performers and gifted instructors, for collaboration in every phase of the original work, *Trampoline Tumbling* of which *Trampoline Tumbling Today* must correctly be considered to be a revision and expansion; Dr. C. H. McCloy, esteemed friend and teacher, whose guidance in classroom and gymnasium has equipped Larry Griswold with any qualifications he may claim as the co-author of this book, and whose expert aid and advice in the preparation of material dealing with body mechanics was invaluable; Hartley D. Price, Newt Loken and Charlie Pond, for their help in compilation of nomenclature, exercise outlines and safety techniques; Bob Fenner, Bill Sorenson, Dick Holzaepfel, George Nissen and Don Carney for their welcome suggestions, and for allowing us to research their private libraries, film studies, and other visual aid materials that were the basis for the new illustrations; Jeff Hennessy, for valuable advice and information regarding international competition and rules; Robert Bollinger, for the Axial Rotation System of rating difficulty, which we recognize as an important contribution to the sport; Harold Frey, whose constructive ideas and discerning counsel have given us a deeper insight into certain phases of the teaching of gymnastics; Members of the National Association of College Gymnastics Coaches for their assistance in practical application of techniques; Business Collaboratores, Inc., St. Louis and Thomas Yoseloff Ltd., Cranbury, N. J., for their perceptive and constructive cooperation in the revision, illustration, and production of this book—*Trampoline Tumbling Today.*

Larry Griswold and Glenn Wilson

Trampoline Tumbling Today

1

History and Development

A brief survey of the trampoline's background and antecedents, the story of why and how it came to be . . . together with a short discussion of trampoline tumbling, its transition from a professional occupation to an amateur sport, and its place in the modern physical education program.

The trampoline is undeniably a newcomer to physical education. It did not, however, spring into being over night. It is the end result of evolution, rather than invention—it is the product of a process of development which covers a period of centuries. It had its beginnings in one of man's oldest and most universal desires—the timeless and inherent urge to overcome gravity.

Among the ancients, this desire led to expression in many ways. Story tellers found it food for dreams—dreams that took form as myths and legends, wherein men flew like birds, soared on magic carpets, or strode with seven-league boots. Savants made it the subject of discourse and experiment. But acrobats and tumblers, popular entertainers since the dawn of history, made of it a source of livelihood—for their appeal to their audiences was based in large measure upon their ability to defeat, if only momentarily, this force which held men earth-bound.

These early entertainers realized the nature and importance of this appeal, and so at an early date, set about to devise and perfect various types of apparatus which would enable them to perform more spectacular feats—which would give them added lift and spring, and allow them to overcome gravity with greater ease and for longer periods.

One of the first devices for this purpose was the springboard, which allowed the performer to leap higher with less effort, and thus perform many heretofore impossible feats of acrobatics. Another early piece of apparatus which saw considerable use was called the "leaps," and consisted of a flexible plank, supported well clear of the ground by blocks at either end. This device enabled the performer to execute a succession of varied acrobatic feats, landing on and rebounding from the resilient plank. However, both the springboard and the "leaps" had obvious disadvantages, which limited and restricted their use.

Seeking to improve upon these early devices, many acrobats and tumblers continued to experiment with various types of springboards, catapults, and the like. Prominent among them, according to circus lore, was a professional performer named Du Trampoline, who first saw the possibility of adapting the safety nets used by aerialists for this purpose. Du Trampoline experimented with crude systems of spring suspension, reduced the size of the net for practicability, and developed the earliest form of the apparatus now called the trampoline.

For many years, the use of the trampoline was confined to professional circles, and there was little recognition of its potentialities with regard to physical education. During this period, however, many outstanding professional performers contributed much to trampoline tumbling—developing and introducing new movements, perfecting techniques, and popularizing the sport through their performances. Some of these men were conscientious teachers as well as expert performers, and engendered an enthusiasm for the new sport among amateur tumblers and gymnastic instructors, influencing many coaches of diving and tumbling to include trampoline tumbling in their programs as early as 1926.

Outstanding among these performers was Tommy Gordon, whose remarkable work made him an almost legendary figure in acrobatic history. His regular performances included double somersaults with half or full twists "in swing," and he ordinarily finished a routine with a forward or backward triple somersault.

Another truly remarkable performer of the first quarter of this century was Joe E. Brown, the movie comedian, who accomplished a full twisting triple backward somersault, a "stunt" which had not been duplicated until 1968, 40 years later.

Other trampoline "greats" of the same and later periods were Stan Stanley, Walter Linsley, Mark Germaine, Bob Orth, Frank Johnson of the Monroe Brothers, Felix Moralis, Antonio Borza, George Paul, and Chuck Keeney, one of our foremost authorities on the sport.

Physical educators, who observed the physical benefits which trampolining produced and who marked particularly the enthusiasm of those who participated, lost little time in introducing the activity into scholastic circles. During World War II it received real impetus through its role in the training of pilots and air crews rapidly and in large numbers. Since 1946 the sport has flourished dramatically, enjoying international recognition as the most popular gymnastic activity ever devised.

Modern equipment and scientific teaching have enabled the amateur trampolinists of today to execute with confidence complicated maneuvers previously considered "impossible." There is little doubt in the minds of the writers that the contestants listed rank in the championship class with those mentioned above, and that they are, with their coaches, continuing to write the history of trampoline tumbling.

2

Notes for the Instructor

A relatively new physical education activity, trampoline tumbling presents the instructor with new problems and new opportunities. Certain explanations, recommendations, and suggestions are offered below, in the hope that they may assist the instructor in solving these problems and in making the most of these opportunities.

DEFINITIONS—Since many of the techniques encountered in trampoline tumbling are similar to those employed in ground tumbling and diving, much of the terminology used to describe movements and exercises is the same for all three sports. However, certain new terms peculiar to trampoline tumbling have evolved; and some terms commonly used in connection with ground tumbling and diving have required special usages when employed with reference to this new sport.

To avoid confusion and to insure consistency, certain of these terms which are either new or have special meanings are listed and defined below.

BODY POSITIONS

LAYOUT—Position of the body in full extension.

TUCK—Position of the body with hips and knees fully flexed, hands clasping shins.

PIKE—Position of the body with hips well flexed, legs straight, knees locked.

Closed pike: hands clasping the under sides of the legs just below the knees.

Open pike: arms extended sidewards.

Jacknife pike: arms forward, hands contacting feet.

FREE—Term indicating that any of the above positions or variations of them is the choice of the performer.

ARCH-OUT—Position of the body is hyperextension, back arched; an example of a free position.

TRAMPOLINE TERMS IN GENERAL USE

BACK—Backward somersault.

BACKOVER—Backward somersaulting action from any position.

BALL-OUT—Forward somersaulting action from back-drop take-off.

BARANI (BARANY, BRANNY) —One-half twisting forward somersault without losing sight of the bed.

BARANI BALL-OUT—Barani from back-drop, to feet.

BARANI IN—Front fliffis with $1/2$ twist in the first somersault.

BARANI OUT—Barani finish of a fliffis or triffis.

BARREL ROLL—Seat-drop, full twist, seat-drop.

BED—The jumping surface of the trampoline.

BED SET—Tautness, softness, or hardness, largely governed by spring tension.

BLIND—Indicating performer cannot see the bed throughout a substantial portion of the stunt.

BLUCH—One-half turntable.

BREAK, BREAKING—Preventing or "killing" rebound by flexing knees to absorb recoil of bed. Also, an interruption in performance of a routine.

BUILD-UP—The use of preparatory bounces to obtain height and control.

CAST—An off-balance take-off, resulting from faulty bed set or faulty body mechanics.

CAT TWIST—Back-drop, full twist, back-drop.

CHECK, CHECKING—Slowing or stopping rotary motion.

CHECK POINT—A focal sighting point for establishing one's relative body position in rotary and twisting movements.

CODY—Backward or forward somersaulting action from the front-drop take-off.

COME-OUT—Extending body and checking rotation preparatory to landing.

CRADLE—Back-drop, 1/2 twisting 1/2 forward somersault, back-drop.

CRASH DIVE—A layout or an arch-out 3/4 front somersault with a last instant ducking of the head before landing on back.

DISMOUNT—Technique of getting off the trampoline.

DOUBLE BOUNCE—The coordinated assistance one performer gives another by helping to depress the bed.

EXERCISE—Stunt, skill, trick, move.

FLIFFIS— (FLIFFES, plural) —Double somersault with at least one-half twist, front or back.

FLYING SOMERSAULT—Somersault is started in layout position and converted to tuck or pike, front or back.

FREE BOUNCE—Straight bounce before executing a stunt.

FRONT—Forward somersault.

FRONT ONE AND THREE—Forward 1 3/4 somersaults to back-drop.

FRONT FULL—Forward somersault with one complete twist.

FULL—Backward somersault with one complete twist.

FULL AND A HALF—Forward somersault with 1 1/2 twists.

GAIN—To travel forward on the bed during the execution of a stunt.

HAND SPOT—Assistance given by a spotter with his hands.

HALF BACK—Term commonly used denoting a 3/4 back somersault to front-drop.

KABOOM—Backward somersaulting action from a unique back-drop take-off.

KICK-OUT—Extending from tuck to pike position.

KIP—*See* Double Bounce. Also, the coordinated thrust from back-drop take-off to gain height and rotation.

MECHANIC—Safety belt, suspended by ropes and pulleys from overhead supports.

MOUNT—Beginning exercise of a routine. Getting onto the bed.

MOVE—Exercise.

OVER—Denotes turning on the lateral axis more than intended or necessary.

PIKE JUMP—A free bounce during which the body assumes a pike position with legs parallel to the bed.

RANDOLPH—Forward somersault with 2½ twists.

ROUTINE—A combination of exercises performed in succession (in swing).

RUDOLPH (RUDY)—Forward somersault with 1½ twists.

SET—Routine.

SHORT—Denotes turning on the lateral axis less than intended or necessary.

SIDE—Side somersault, rotating on the dorso-ventral axis.

SPOT, SPOTTING—Executing take-off and landing on the same spot on the bed. To protect or assist a performer doing a stunt or routine.

SPOTTER—One who protects or spots a performer.

STRADDLE PIKE BOUNCE—Pike Bounce with legs spread apart, arms forward with hands touching in-steps.

SWING, SWINGTIME—Doing routine with no free bounces.

SWIVEL HIPS—Seat-drop, ½ twist, seat-drop.

TRAMPOLINING—Trampoline tumbling.

TRAVEL—To move from one area of the bed to another.

TRIFFIS—Triple somersault with one-half or more twists.

TURNTABLE—Front-drop, side somersault, front-drop.

TWIST—Rotation of the body on its longitudinal axis.

TWISTING BELT—Specially designed belt that facilitates the spotting of twisting stunts.

WHIP BACK—Fast low somersault in layout or arch-out position.

WORKING THE BED—Coordination of the various actions required to obtain maximum lift from the bed without loss of control.

WRAP, WRAP-UP—Action of the arms being drawn in close to body, to speed twisting rotation.

GENERAL SUGGESTIONS—As has been said before, certain of the techniques employed in trampoline tumbling are fundamentally identical with those involved in ground tumbling and diving. However, despite basic similarities, these techniques require marked and important modification when applied on the trampoline. Therefore, it is imperative that all students, no matter how expert they may be on the tumbling mat or springboard, undergo a period of training in the fundamentals of trampoline tumbling.

It is strongly recommended that the first few periods of instruction embrace nothing beyond the discussion and demonstration of fundamental body mechanics, and practice in the execution of the seven fundamental bounces—singly and in combination.

During this fundamental period, the student not only learns the basic techniques, but is also afforded an opportunity to perfect them to the point where he instinctively adjusts balance, checks overthrow, and works the bed without waste effort and with practiced coordination.

In trampoline tumbling, it is imperative that both the instructor and the student keep constantly in mind the fact that *spotting every bounce and every exercise*—executing take-off and landing on the same spot—is of paramount importance. It is the criterion of good trampoline tumbling, and is so vital to controlled execution of all movements that one can never consider an exercise learned until able to spot it consistently. The student is never ready to proceed to any advanced step until he can spot all previous work. It is up to the instructor to insist upon strict attention to spotting, and to the student to charge himself with its perfection.

The well-managed trampoline class moves along smoothly and rapidly if a few simple rules are followed.

Allow only one person at a time on the trampoline—at least until the individuals become proficient in their skills.

Allow each student approximately 30 seconds for each turn on the trampoline. Longer turns tend to lessen class interest.

Keep the class group small, allowing more time per student. If the enrollment is large, the class may be divided into several squads, and while one squad issuing the trampoline the others can be using other gymnasium equipment. The squads may then be rotated through the various activities.

Wearing apparel should consist of T-shirt, trunks, and regulation gymnastic shoes or heavy socks. No tennis shoes or other type shoes should be worn as they cause excessive wear on the trampoline bed. Mat burns may result from improper landings on elbows and knees. It is recommended that sweat shirts be worn until correct landings are mastered.

Mounting and dismounting properly should be a strict rule from the very beginning. The student climbs onto

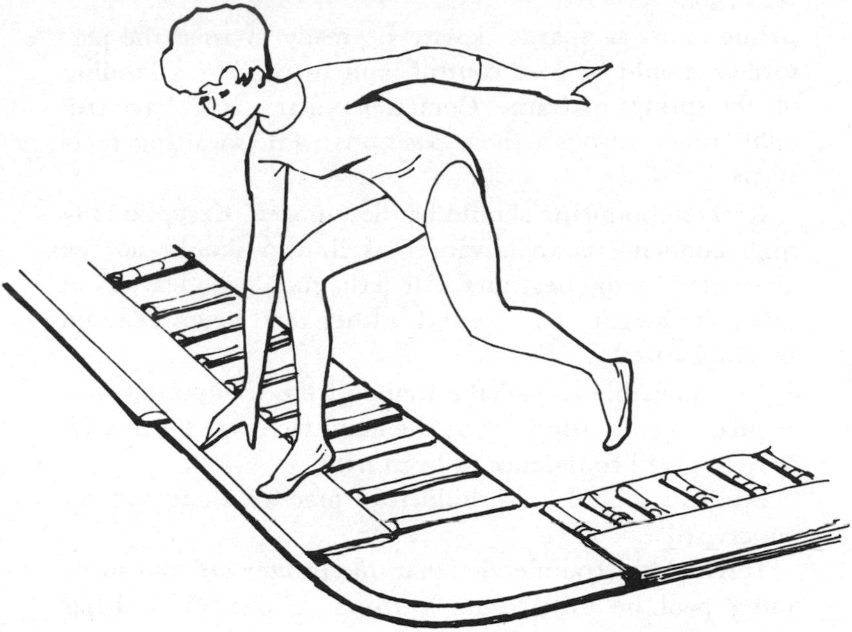

the trampoline by placing his hands on the frame and stepping up onto the frame, across the springs, and onto the bed. He should always place the hands on the frame while mounting or dismounting. To dismount, the student should walk to the end or side of the bed, bend over and place one hand on the frame, then step from the bed to the frame and to the floor. He should not bounce from the bed to the floor. Breaking, or checking the bounce, should be taught at the first opportunity and stressed as a safety measure. The student should break whenever he starts to lose balance or control. This is done by simply flexing the knees sharply upon landing, absorbing the upward thrust of the bed. This enables the performer to stop suddenly and avoid dangerous rebounding.

During instruction or practice periods, members of the class should be stationed at the ends and sides of the trampoline to act as guards (spotters), ready to assist the performer should he lose control, and to prevent a landing on the springs or frame. Common practice is to have students rotate through these positions while awaiting their turns.

Reckless bouncing should be discouraged. Exceptionally high bouncing is an advanced skill, and should not be attempted by the beginner. All skills should be learned at moderate heights, and control, rather than height, should be emphasized.

It is advisable to pad the frame of the trampoline with regulation pads, supplied by the manufacturer. These pads help to instill confidence in beginners.

Students should be forbidden to practice alone and unsupervised.

It is highly recommended that the springboard and swimming pool be utilized in learning to control multiple twisting somersaults. This method reduces the chances of straining the tendons of the knees and ankles, often caused by imperfect landings during the critical period of practicing newly learned stunts. It offers distinct advantages for timing the come-out, checking the twist, and orientation in mid-air.

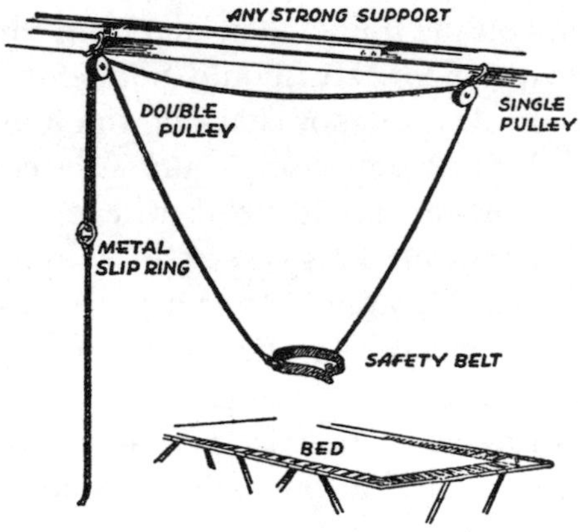

Tumbling belts serve the same purpose in trampoline tumbling as in ground tumbling, and should always be employed in teaching multiple somersaults, twisting movements, and advanced routines. Either regular or suspended safety belts may be used for somersaults. For advanced twisting stunts the "twisting belt" is indispensable. Learning "in the belt" is not only a safety precaution—it goes far toward eliminating mental hazard on the part of the student approaching a new and difficult exercise.

MODEL LESSONS—The following lessons are suggested as examples of instructional procedure. They should follow complete discussion and demonstration of body mechanics.

Lesson No. 1

1. Mounting and dismounting.
   Demonstration and practice of proper techniques.
2. Straight bouncing.
   Demonstration and practice, stressing spotting.
3. Breaking.
   Demonstration and practice, breaking on command.
4. Hands and knees bounce.
   Demonstration and practice, stressing four-point landing alignment.

Lesson No. 2

1. Review and practice of techniques.
2. Knees bounce.
   Half twist to right, to left, to feet, to knees.
3. Seat-drop.
   Repeat in swing.
   Half twist to feet.
   Seat-drop, knees, hands and knees; repeat.

Lesson No. 3

1. Review and practice of skills previously learned.

2. Front-drop.

   To save time and avoid mat burns all members of the class should be requested to assume the front-drop position on the floor while the instructor checks for faults. Suggested progression: From hands and knees bounce the body is extended for the landing in front drop position, and the rebound is made to feet.

3. Practice routine: Hands and knees, front-drop, feet, seat-drop, half twist to feet.

Lesson No. 4

1. Review and practice of learned skills.
2. Back-drop.

   Demonstration, accenting the forward thrust of the hips by arching body as one leg is brought forward from standing (not bouncing) position, and the drop to the back is made with chin held forward to chest, eyes forward on trampoline frame.

   Spotting this skill is most important.

   Demonstration of back-drop with low bounce and practice on both techniques.

Lesson No. 5

1. Review of all skills learned, encouraging original routines based upon them.
2. Hands bounce.

   This is a particularly fine skill for conditioning arms and shoulders. Although it is difficult for many beginners to learn, and is often omitted in the younger student's program, it is a favorite exercise of the complete trampoline tumbler and the all-around gymnast.

Lesson No. 6

1. Swivel-hips.

   Suggested progression:

   Seat-drop, feet, half twist; repeat.

Seat-drop, half twist to feet; repeat.
Seat-drop, half twist to seat-drop.

2. Half turntable.

Lesson No. 7

1. Forward somersault.
   Progressions: See Basic Exercises 3, 4 and 5.

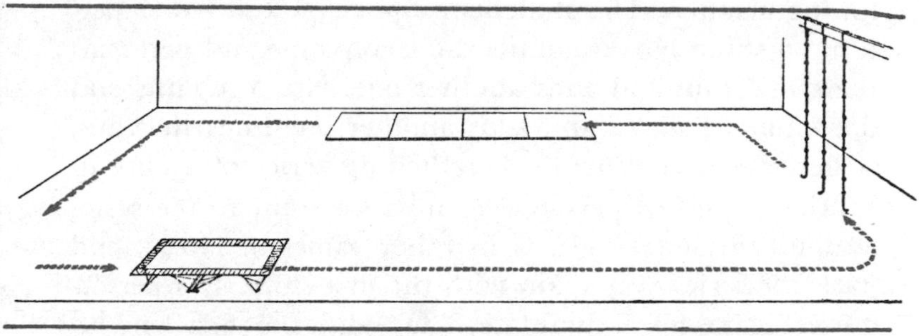

Suggested arrangement with two additional pieces of apparatus

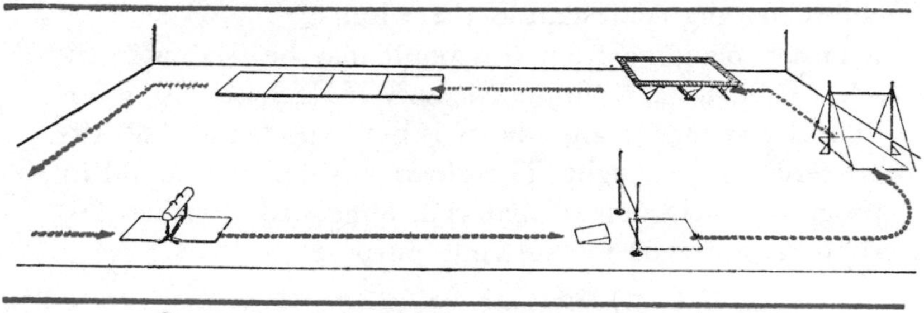

Suggested arrangement with four additional pieces of apparatus

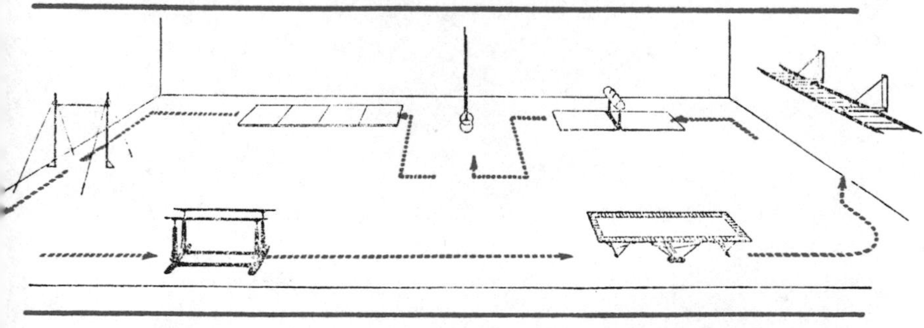

Suggested arrangement with five additional pieces of apparatus

Lesson No. 8

The student should now be encouraged to design and organize routines with emphasis upon good form. The instructor may judge or grade the students and arrange groupings for further instruction accordingly.

To stimulate interest in competition the game of "Trampoline Horse" may be introduced. It is played in the following manner: The students number off and No. 1 performs a stunt. No. 2 mounts the trampoline and performs the same stunt and adds another one. No. 3 mounts and does stunts 1 and 2 and adds another one himself. Thus, it becomes a continually lengthening series of stunts in routine. The first person who misses a stunt in the series assumes the letter "H" as in other games of Horse, and starts the series over again with the first stunt. If a person misses again he accumulates "O" and the first one to accumulate H-O-R-S-E is eliminated from the game. The last remaining contestant is the winner.

Lesson planning from this point may be facilitated by selecting material from the Glossary of Exercises, using the difficulty ratings as a guide. It is not expected that all exercises listed be taught. The glossary is designed to aid in progressive selection of material. Suggested Routines are similarly arranged for the same purpose.

3

Fundamental Body Mechanics

Both an understanding of the fundamental principles of body mechanics involved in trampoline tumbling and a knowledge of the specific manner in which these principles are applied are essential to proficient performance on the trampoline. Certain of these basic actions—those with most general applications—are discussed and illustrated in the section which follows.

In the performance of any task, a knowledge of the basic techniques involved in its execution is essential. And this knowledge attains full utility only when it is based upon an adequate understanding of how these specific techniques, methods, and procedures relate to the task at hand—of how and why they operate to produce desired results. Nowhere do these elementary facts have greater application than in trampoline tumbling.

The various exercises and routines performed by the trampoline tumbler are nothing more than the combined execution of a variety of specific techniques—techniques which enable the performer to twist, bounce, spin, etc. These techniques, in turn, are the products of the coordinated employment of certain body actions which enable the performer to initiate, direct, or arrest motion. Basically, this is the essence of trampoline tumbling.

But, as in skiing, diving, flying, hurdling, or any other active sport, the various actions which together constitute techniques of execution must be performed rapidly. Coordination of these actions must be instantaneous, automatic—almost instinctive. Once committed, the performer has no time for debate, consideration, or reflection. His actions must be immediate, uninterrupted, and unfailingly correct. He is reliant upon muscle memory, rather than will—in short, his thinking must be done beforehand. The various body actions which make possible the techniques he employs must be so thoroughly known and understood as to partake of the nature of reflexes, rather than consciously directed movements.

It was with this thought in mind that the following pages were prepared. Specifically, this section deals with fundamental body mechanics—with the manner in which various parts of the body are brought into play to control movement. Its function is to acquaint both the instructor and the student with certain of those fundamental actions which combine to form the basic techniques employed in trampoline tumbling. By means of illustrations and discussion, the relationships of body mechanics to the various techinques used in executing exercises and routines on the trampoline are explained and emphasized, as the first step toward the establishment of an adequate foundation for proficient performance.

The resilient bed of the trampoline, which absorbs the impact of the performer's body and converts this force of impact into recoil, presents the trampoline tumbler with certain fundamental requirements. On landing, he must transmit as much of his momentum as possible to the bed to insure adequate recoil. During the take-off, he must absorb as much of the recoil force as possible to insure a sufficiently high rebound. In addition, he must contact and leave the bed in such a manner as to minimize shock and jar, and, in most cases, avoid all cast and travel.

In studying these illustrations, it will be noted that

FUNDAMENTAL BODY POSITIONS

NO. 1

(Body Mechanics)

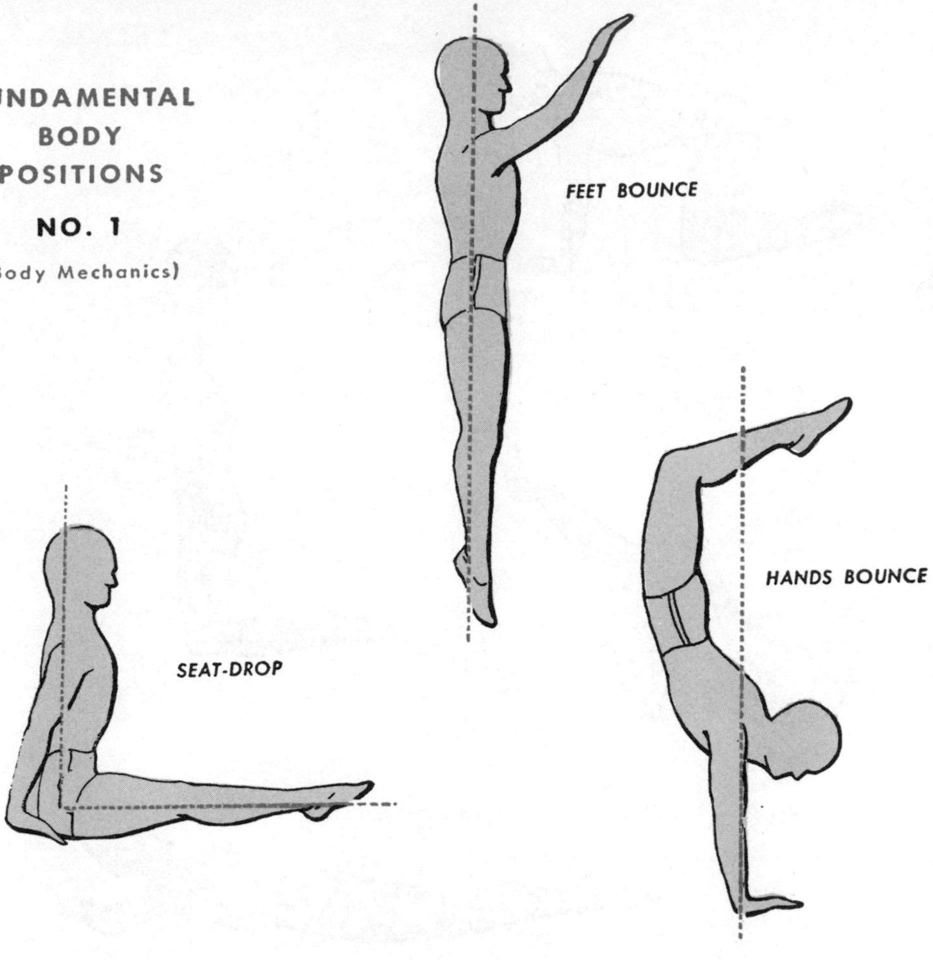

where the major portion of the body is held erect, and contact with the bed is made on relatively small supporting surfaces, such as the feet, seat, or knees, the body structure is so aligned as to keep the forces of impact or recoil on a line perpendicular to the bed surface. Thus, the maximum amount of force may be imparted to or absorbed from the bed; and the rigid vertical alignment prevents body-snap or bending upon impact, and elim-

inates cast on take-off. Alignment may be altered to initiate rotation.

In those positions where the major portion of the body lies in a horizontal position and contact is made over relatively large surfaces, alignment is maintained parallel to the surface of the bed. This allows the forces of impact and recoil to be exerted and absorbed evenly over the area of contact, again preventing snap and cast.

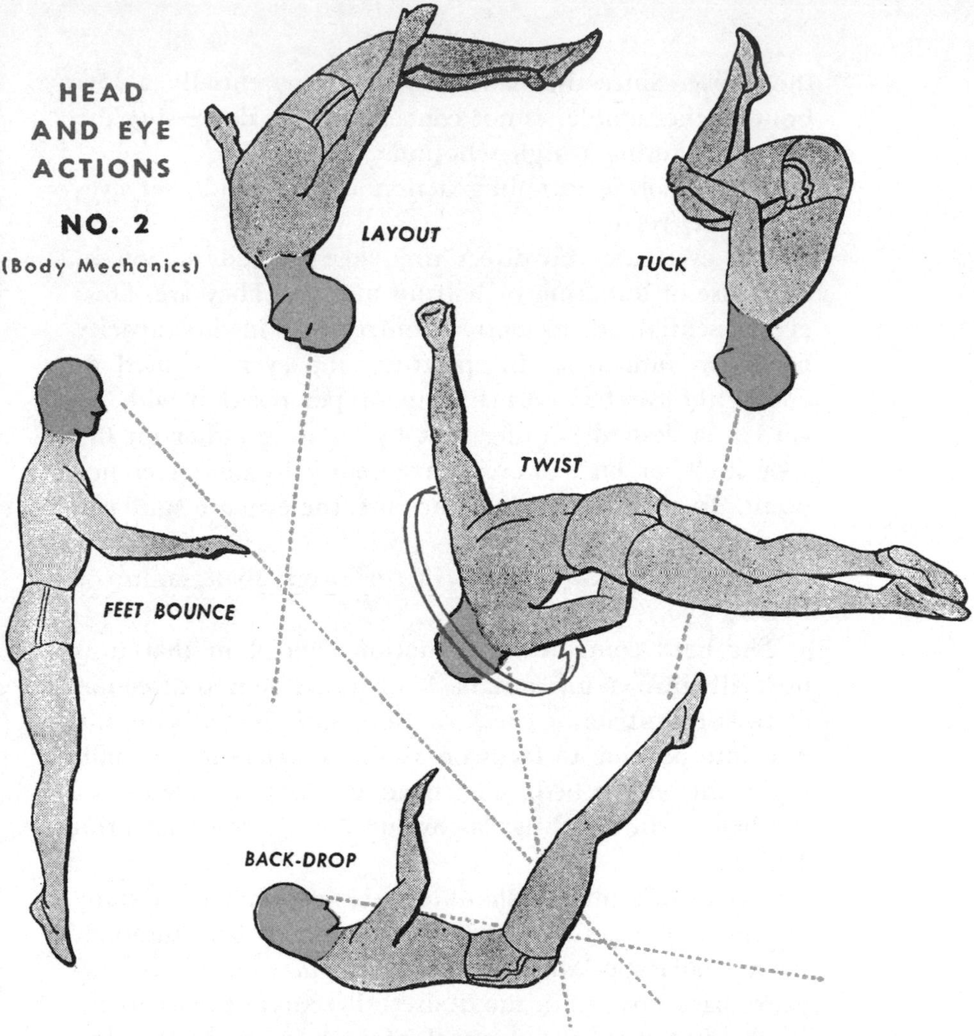

The hands and knees position involves a combination of both vertical and horizontal alignment. That portion of the body between the shoulders and the hips lies horizontally, and alignment is parallel to the bed. The arms and thighs, however, act as supporting pillars between this portion of the body and the points of contact, and alignment here is vertical.

The hands-bounce position is the single exception to

the above. Since the hands bounce is essentially a low bounce, the tumbler is not concerned with depressing the bed or attaining a high rebound.

In trampoline tumbling action of the head and eyes are closely related.

The eyes exert no direct influence on body action in the sense of initiating or halting motion. They are, however, essential aids to motion control, and in this capacity have two functions. In spottting, the eyes are used to enable the tumbler to maintain proper position with regard to a desired landing spot by focusing either on the spot itself, or on a more conveniently located reference point. In checking, or in come-outs, the eyes are similarly used to determine the point at which rotation should be slowed or a come-out made in turnovers, somersaults, or twists.

The head contributes to motion control in that it is normally thrown forward, back, or in the desired direction of twist to initiate or check motion, and also to bring the eyes into position to focus on a desired reference or landing point on the bed. The head is always kept clear of the bed during landings, as exemplified in the back-drop position.

Actions of arms and shoulders are vital factors in many of the techniques employed by the trampoline tumbler.

Generally speaking, the shoulders may be thrust forward, backward, or in the desired direction of twist to aid in the initiation and control of body motion. In addition, they act as pivot-points for various actions of the arms.

Arm actions may be grouped into general classifications with reference to function. The most important actions of the arms are those employed in the initiation and control of motion. Here the arms are used to maintain balance while floating, to initiate or retard motion in twists

or turnovers, and to add force to landings and impetus to take-offs through reaction or the transfer of momentum. The arms are also used to provide support, as in the seat-drop, and as aids in maintaining and controlling position, as in a tuck or pike.

The amount of control exerted by both arms and shoul-

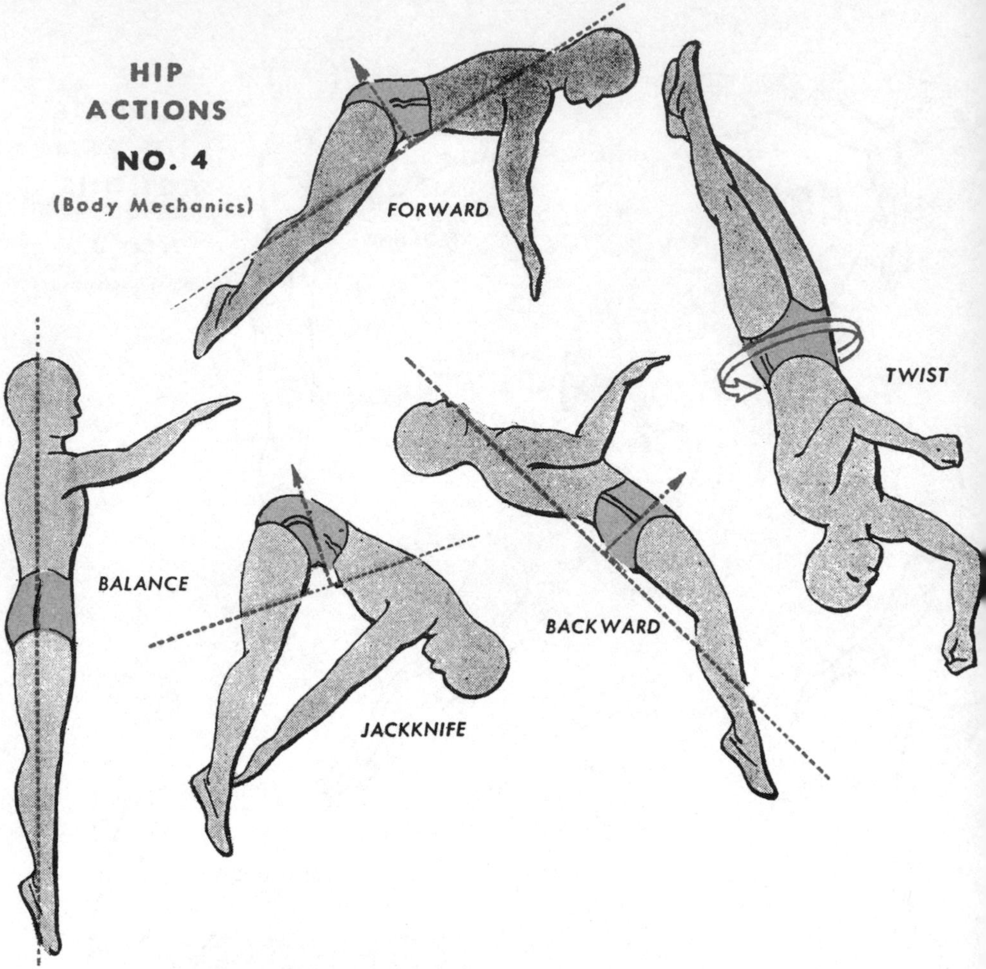

ders depends upon their proper coordination with the actions of other parts of the body.

The hips provide a point of flexion close to the body's center of gravity, and are employed in trampoline tumbling to achieve balance and to direct motion.

In straight up-and-down bouncing, the hips are used to keep the center of gravity on a line perpendicular to the bed, thus insuring that the main forces of landing or recoil are exerted along that line.

LEG AND FOOT ACTIONS

NO. 5
(Body Mechanics)

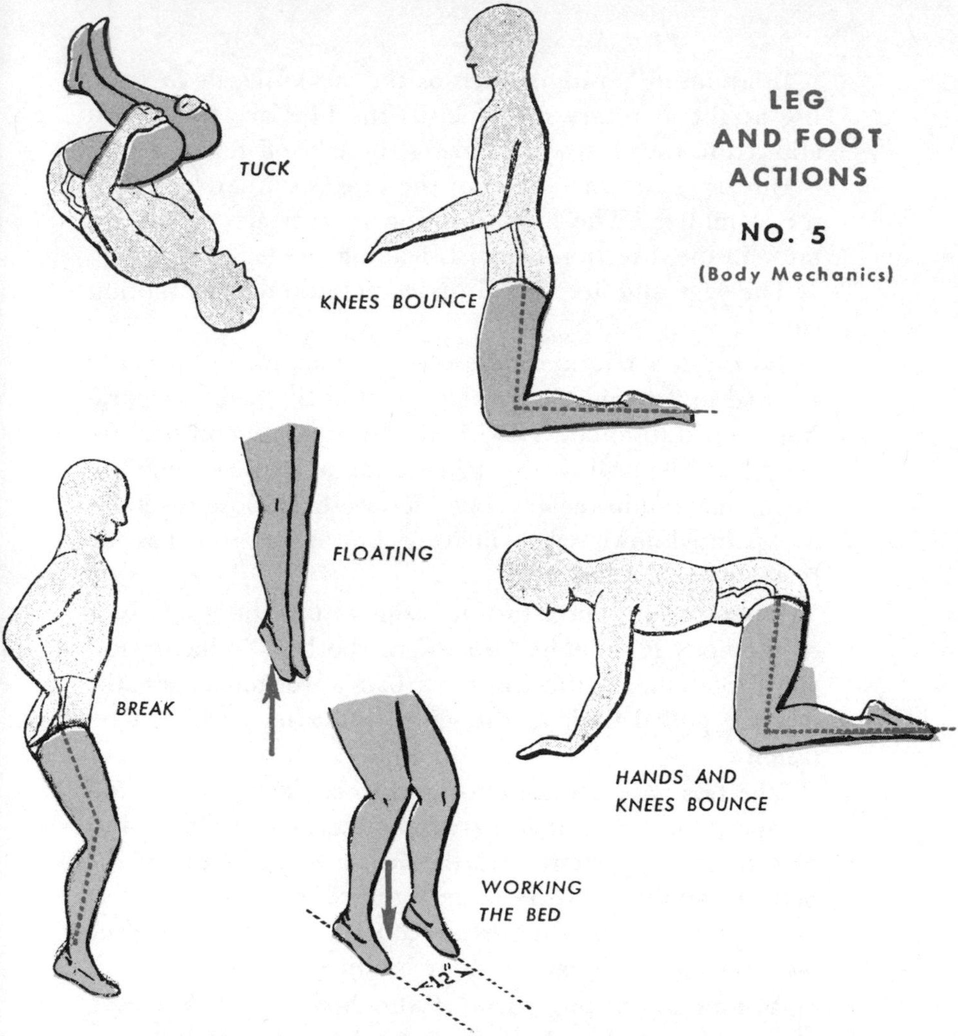

When movements involving forward turnovers or somersaults are executed, the hips are thrust back of this perpendicular line, displacing the center of gravity, and inducing forward rotation as the force of recoil is exerted upon the body. Hips are thrust forward of this line in executing backovers and backward somersaults, inducing backward rotation.

In assuming positions such as the jackknife, or in gaining height in rotary movements, the hips are flexed and allowed to travel upward during the take-off impulse.

During twists, the action of the hips is similar to that of the shoulders. The hips, reacting to arm action, are rotated in the direction of twist, leading the legs.

The legs and feet are important adjuncts to motion control.

To break a bounce and prevent rebound, the legs are allowed to flex and absorb the recoil of the bed. In working the bed to obtain maximum lift, the legs and feet are extended, depressing the bed as far as possible and insuring maximum recoil. The feet are held close together, toes pointed down, while floating, but are separated as the feet contact the bed.

When tucking for a forward somersault, the upper part of the body is brought *forward* to the legs, inducing forward rotation. In tucking for a backward somersault, the legs are pulled back to the chest, inducing backward rotation.

The legs and feet are also used to achieve stability and balance. In the hands and knees bounce, four stable points of contact are present, and the feet are kept clear of the bed on landing. In the knees bounce, however, the feet are lowered so that the insteps contact the bed, providing —together with the knees—four landing points.

Actions of various parts of the body—head and eyes, arms and shoulders, hips, legs and feet—are combined to produce movements of the body as a whole. Generally speaking, these body actions take the form of rotary movements on one of the three body-axes—the lateral, or side-to-side, axis; the longitudinal, or head-to-foot, axis; and the dorso-ventral, or front-to-back, axis. Turnovers and somersaults involve rotation on the lateral axis, twists are

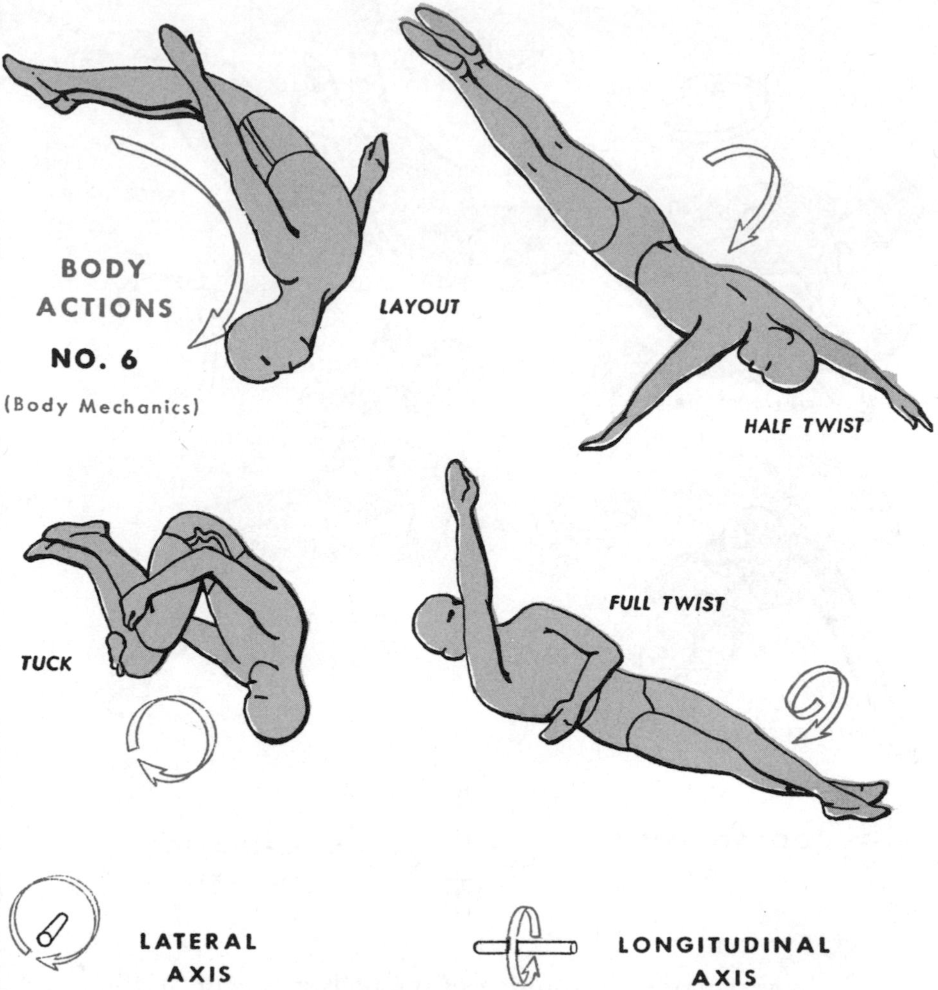

executed on the longitudinal axis, and side-spins on the dorso-ventral axis.

In executing these movements, the actions of various parts of the body are so coordinated as to induce or halt rotation, and to control its speed. Control is achieved

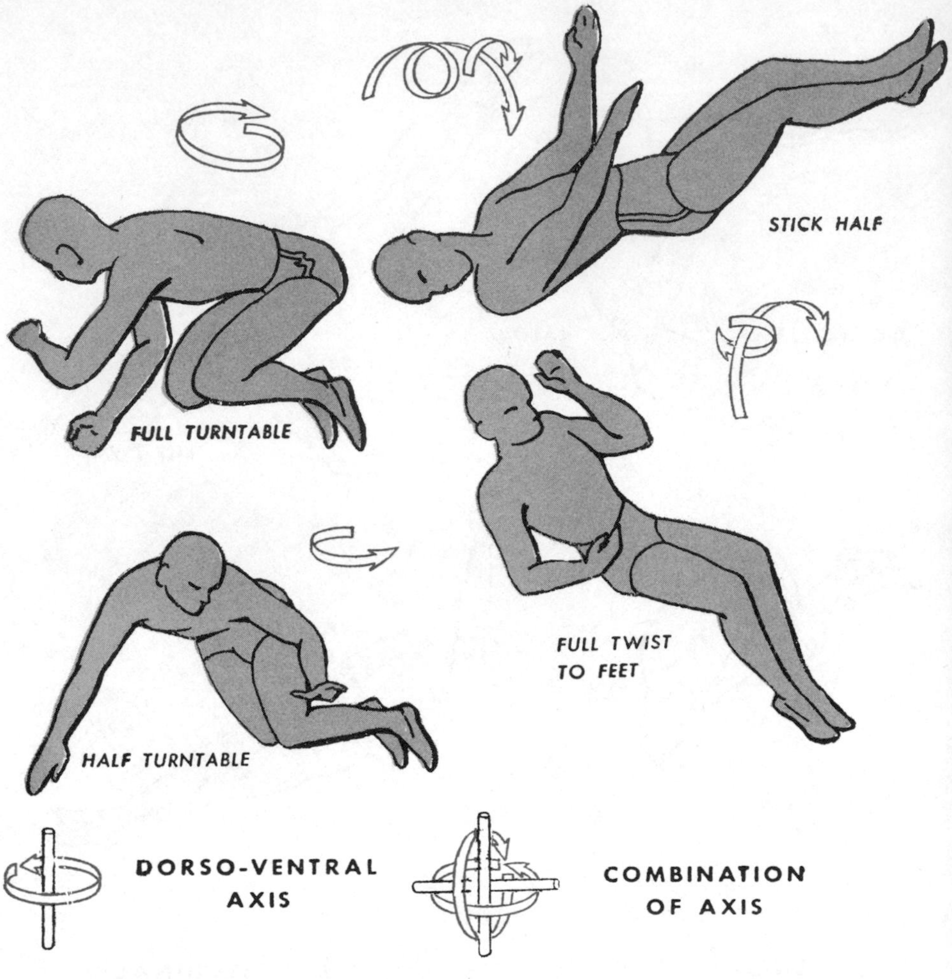

by varying the distribution of the body-mass with relation to the center of rotation, and thus increasing or reducing the moment of inertia—or, in plain language, making it harder or easier to overcome inertia and rotate the body. For example, in a somersault or turnover, a tight tuck position concentrates the body-mass close to the center of rotation, reducing the moment of inertia, and resulting in easier—therefore, faster—rotation. In a layout position, however, the body mass is distributed farther away from the center of rotation; rotation is then more difficult, and therefore, slower.

The same principle is used in controlling twists. The arms are kept close to the body in full twists, to allow easy rotation. In half twists, where a smaller amount of rotation is required, the arms are ordinarily held farther out from the body. Both arms and legs are employed in a similar fashion in the execution of side-spins, or turntables.

Certain body actions are achieved by combined movement on two axes. In the stick half—or backward somersault with half twist—and the back-drop with full twist to feet, illustrated above, movement takes place on both the lateral and longitudinal axes.

4

Simple Demonstrations

. . . by means of which the instructor may indicate and explain what takes place in certain of the more important actions encountered in trampoline tumbling.

Trampoline tumbling is a dynamic sport—the tumbler is in motion and must act while in motion. Static words and pictures may serve to indicate the actions involved and explain how they are performed—but the reasons why certain body actions produce certain desired results can best be illustrated by dynamic demonstration.

Conscientious instructors realize that a thorough knowledge of "reasons why" is the cornerstone of complete understanding, but are often handicapped by the lack of suitable and convenient means to implement this phase of instruction. Fortunately, many of the "reasons why" involved in trampoline tumbling can be adequately illustrated and explained through demonstrations which require only a few simple, easily-constructed "props", assembled and utilized as shown below and on succeeding pages.

To DEMONSTRATE *why* *the trampoline tumbler can bounce straight up and down, taking off and landing at the same spot on the bed:*

2

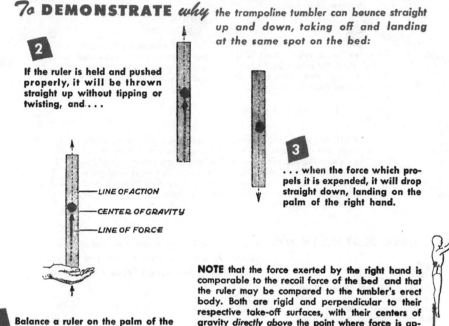

If the ruler is held and pushed properly, it will be thrown straight up without tipping or twisting, and . . .

3

. . . when the force which propels it is expended, it will drop straight down, landing on the palm of the right hand.

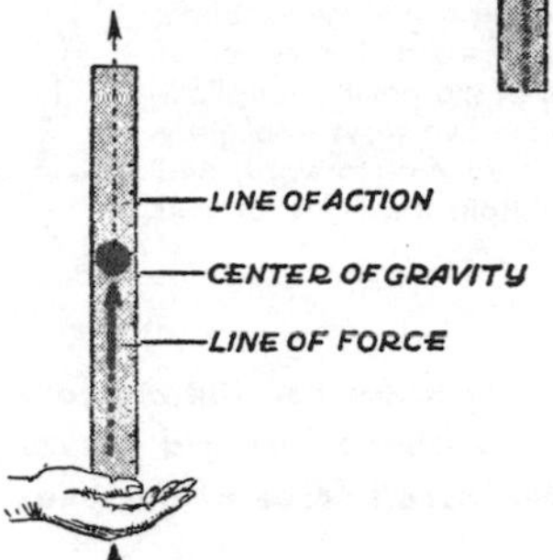

1

Balance a ruler on the palm of the right hand, with its long axis perpendicular to the upturned palm. Use the left hand to steady and guide the ruler as the right hand pushes it sharply and directly upward.

NOTE that the force exerted by the right hand is comparable to the recoil force of the bed and that the ruler may be compared to the tumbler's erect body. Both are rigid and perpendicular to their respective take-off surfaces, with their centers of gravity *directly above* the point where force is applied. Thus, the recoil force of the bed is exerted directly upward against the center of gravity, causing the body to rise along a vertical line.

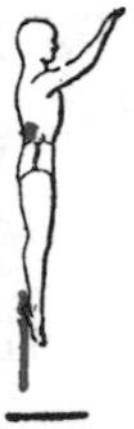

To DEMONSTRATE *why* the trampoline tumbler can initiate forward rotation combined with forward travel by utilizing the recoil force of the bed:

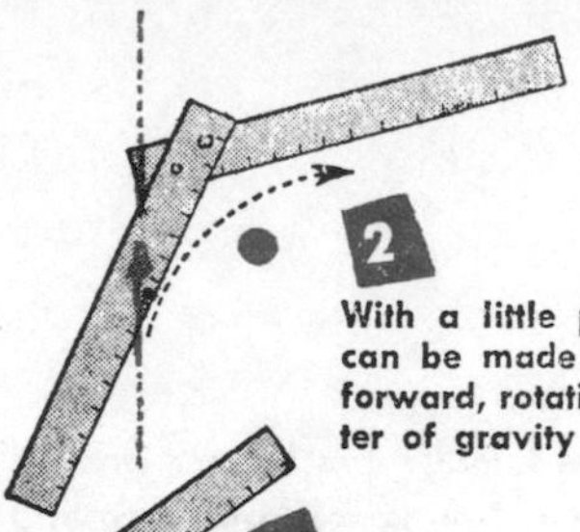
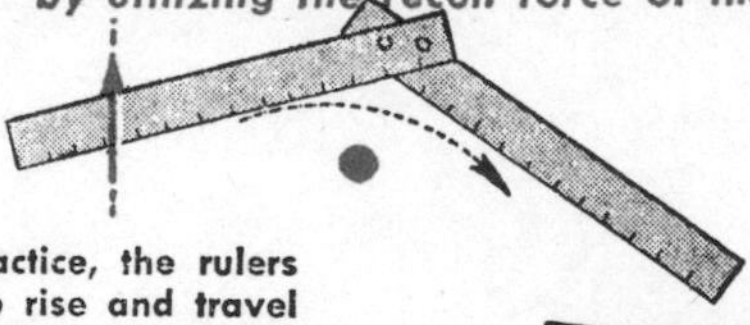

2

With a little practice, the rulers can be made to rise and travel forward, rotating about their center of gravity . . .

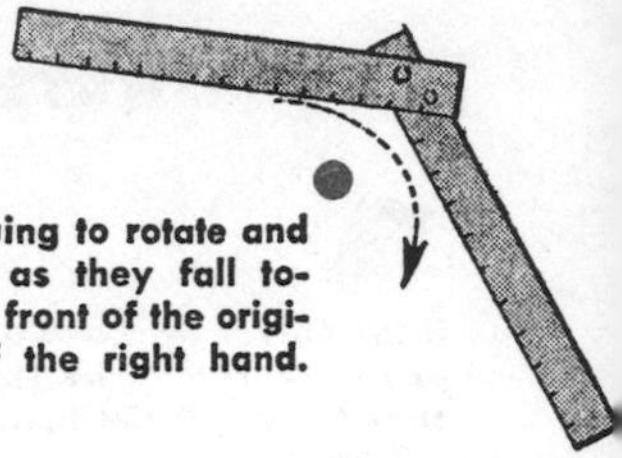

3

. . . and continuing to rotate and travel forward as they fall toward a point in front of the original position of the right hand.

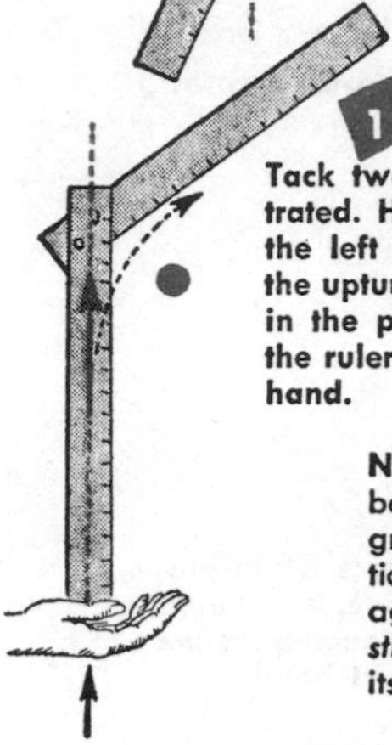

1

Tack two rulers together, as illustrated. Hold the rulers lightly with the left hand, and place them on the upturned palm of the right hand in the position shown. Then push the rulers up sharply with the right hand.

NOTE that the rulers, as assembled here, represent the tumbler's body with hips bent and trunk inclined forward. The center of gravity in this instance is located *in front* of the point of application of force. As a result, the force works in two ways—*obliquely* against the center of gravity, pushing it up and forward, and *straight up* against the hips, tending to spin the body around its center of gravity.

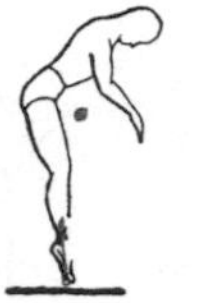

To DEMONSTRATE *why* the trampoline tumbler can initiate forward rotation, without forward travel by utilizing the recoil force of the bed:

2

As the rulers are propelled upward by the right hand and simultaneously released by the left hand, ruler B will snap down and forward; and ruler A will push forward against the right hand . . .

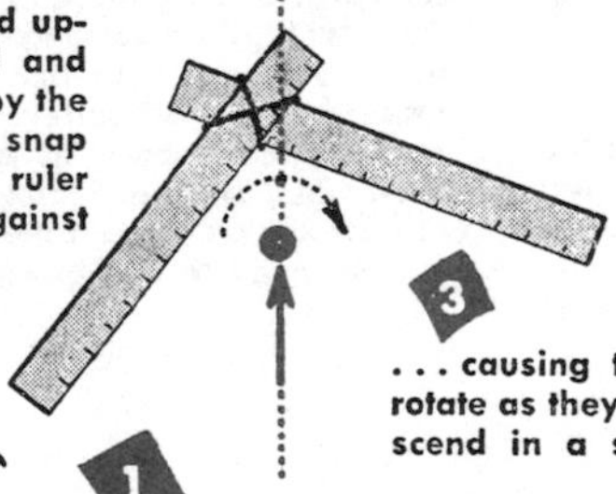
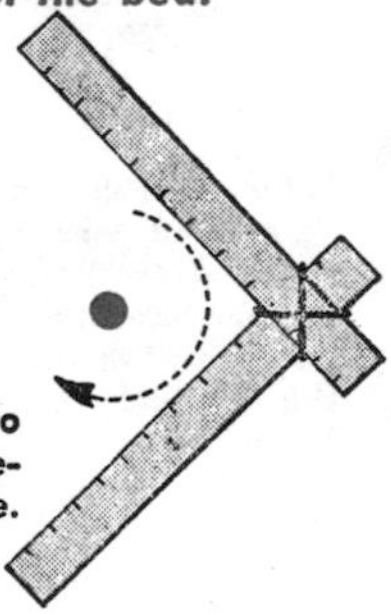

3

. . . causing the rulers to rotate as they rise and descend in a straight line.

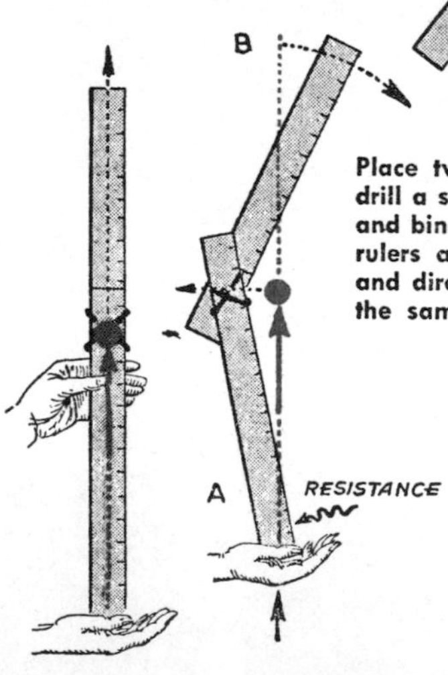

1

Place two rulers as illustrated above, and drill a small hole through both. Insert a nail and bind rulers with rubber bands. Hold the rulers as shown at left, and push sharply and directly upward, releasing the rulers at the same time.

NOTE that the action of the rulers when released approximates the action of the tumbler's body when he bends at the hips, and pushes forward with his feet as he leaves the bed. Here the center of gravity is located *in front* of the body, but is still *directly* over the point of application of force. Thus, the center of gravity rises vertically, and there is no forward travel. The momentum of the head and shoulders and reaction from the forward push delivered by the feet cause the body to rotate about its moving center of gravity.

To DEMONSTRATE *why* *the trampoline tumbler can initiate motion through the transfer of momentum:*

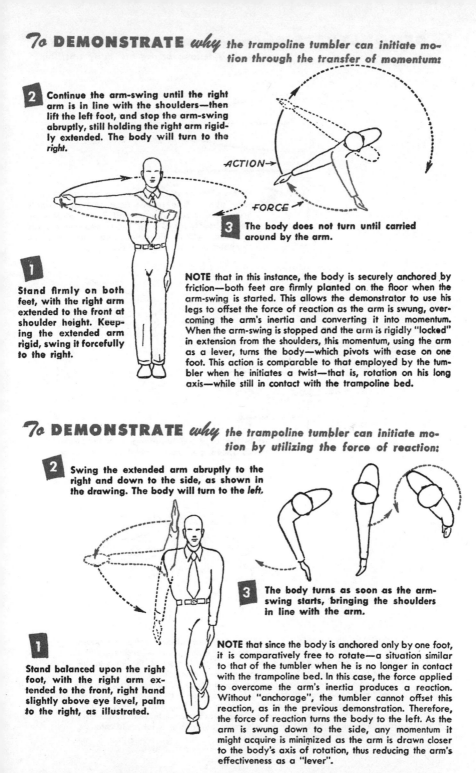

2 **Continue the arm-swing until the right arm is in line with the shoulders—then lift the left foot, and stop the arm-swing abruptly, still holding the right arm rigidly extended. The body will turn to the *right.***

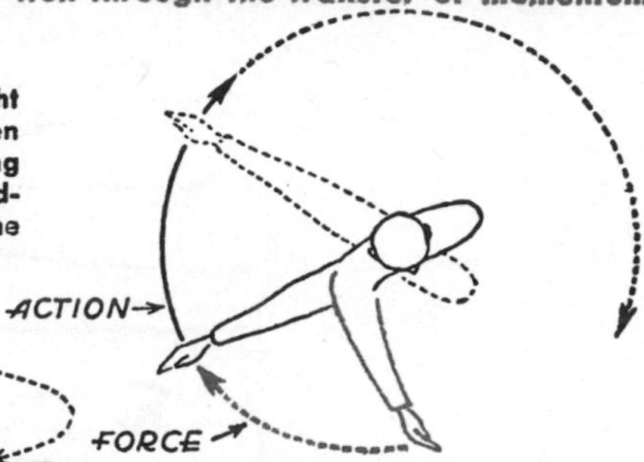

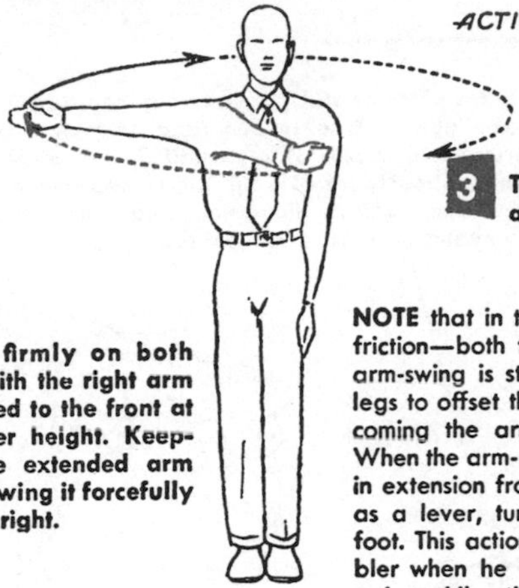

3 **The body does not turn until carried around by the arm.**

1 **Stand firmly on both feet, with the right arm extended to the front at shoulder height. Keeping the extended arm rigid, swing it forcefully to the right.**

NOTE that in this instance, the body is securely anchored by friction—both feet are firmly planted on the floor when the arm-swing is started. This allows the demonstrator to use his legs to offset the force of reaction as the arm is swung, overcoming the arm's inertia and converting it into momentum. When the arm-swing is stopped and the arm is rigidly "locked" in extension from the shoulders, this momentum, using the arm as a lever, turns the body—which pivots with ease on one foot. This action is comparable to that employed by the tumbler when he initiates a twist—that is, rotation on his long axis—while still in contact with the trampoline bed.

To DEMONSTRATE *why* *the trampoline tumbler can initiate motion by utilizing the force of reaction:*

2 **Swing the extended arm abruptly to the right and down to the side, as shown in the drawing. The body will turn to the *left.***

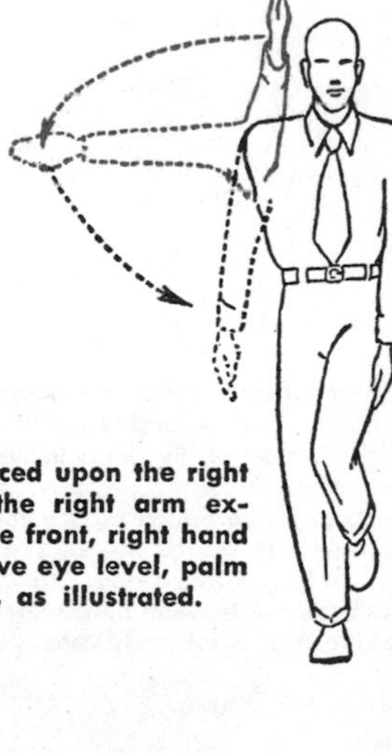

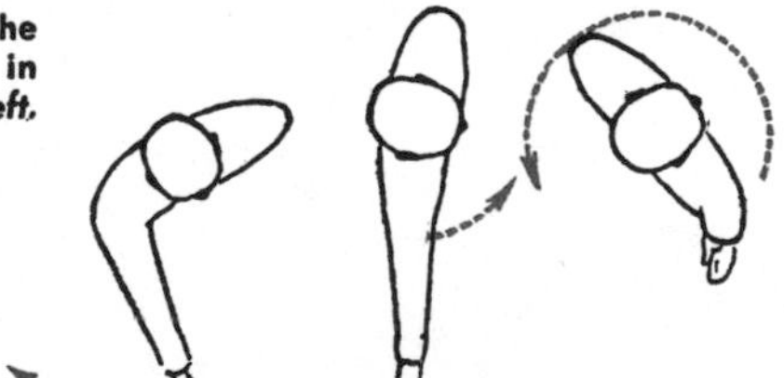

3 **The body turns as soon as the arm-swing starts, bringing the shoulders in line with the arm.**

1 **Stand balanced upon the right foot, with the right arm extended to the front, right hand slightly above eye level, palm to the right, as illustrated.**

NOTE that since the body is anchored only by one foot, it is comparatively free to rotate—a situation similar to that of the tumbler when he is no longer in contact with the trampoline bed. In this case, the force applied to overcome the arm's inertia produces a reaction. Without "anchorage", the tumbler cannot offset this reaction, as in the previous demonstration. Therefore, the force of reaction turns the body to the left. As the arm is swung down to the side, any momentum it might acquire is minimized as the arm is drawn closer to the body's axis of rotation, thus reducing the arm's effectiveness as a "lever".

To DEMONSTRATE *why* *the trampoline tumbler's speed of rotation is influenced by his body position:*

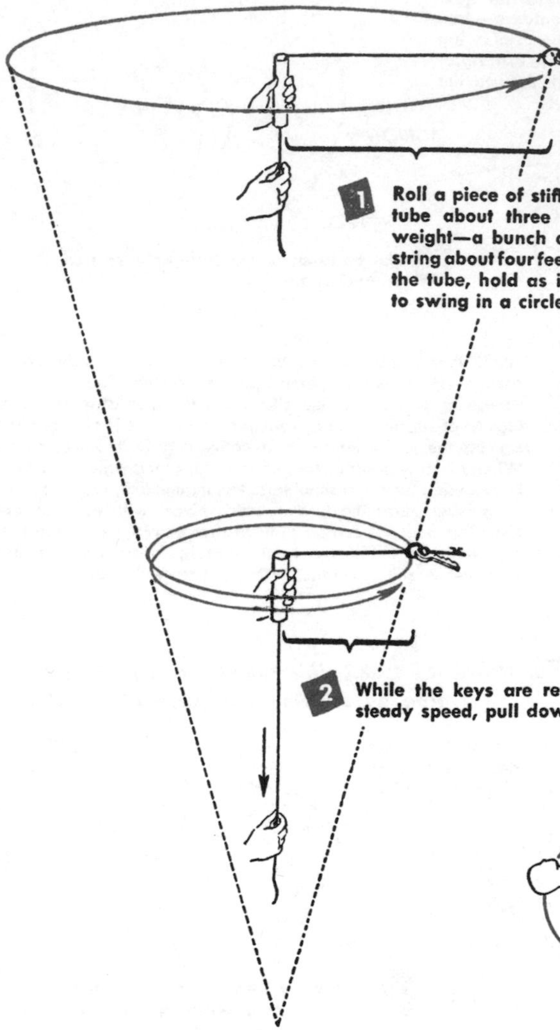

1 **Roll a piece of stiff paper or cardboard to form a tube about three inches long. Attach a small weight—a bunch of keys will do—to a piece of string about four feet long. Thread the string through the tube, hold as illustrated, and cause the keys to swing in a circle around the tube.**

2 **While the keys are revolving at a moderate, steady speed, pull down rapidly on the string.**

NOTE that, as the string is pulled, the radius of rotation is *decreased,* and the rapidity of rotation is *increased.* In other words—considering the illustration above—when the string is pulled (shortened), the keys in the lower picture are making two complete revolutions about the paper tube in the same length of time required by the keys in the upper picture for one revolution. Technically, mass is concentrated closer to the axis of rotation, reducing the moment of inertia, and making rotation easier, and, therefore, more rapid. The tumbler employs this principle when he assumes positions which distribute his body's mass close to its axis for rapid rotation, or far from its axis for slow rotation.

5

The Seven Fundamental Bounces

Mastery of the seven fundamental bounces is the most important single step in learning trampoline tumbling, for they constitute take-off or landing positions for every exercise performed on the trampoline. The following pages are, therefore, devoted to detailed, illustrated instructions for the execution of those coordinated techniques which provide maximum lift and control in each of the seven bounces.

The seven fundamental bounces—feet bounce, hands and knees bounce, knees bounce, seat-drop, front-drop, back-drop, and hands bounce—are undoubtedly the most important set of skills utilized by the trampoline tumbler. They are the key to proficiency, for one or another of these seven bounces serves as the landing or take-off in every exercise or combination of exercises performed in trampoline tumbling.

These seven fundamental bounces may be compared to the take-offs and entries employed in springboard diving—a comparison in which major differences are immediately apparent. In trampoline tumbling, *landings* are made, not entries, and most take-offs are executed without the forward gaining movement encountered in springboard diving. In addition, the diver is limited to one basic type of take-off—one in which his feet make final contact with the springboard—and must make either a head-first or feet-first entry to avoid injury. The trampoline tumbler, on the other hand, may execute any one of seven take-offs, and may select from an equal number of landing positions, thus making possible a wider range of intervening exercises. Moreover, he can perform these exercises individually, in swing, or combined in routines, setting whatever pace he chooses and bringing into concentrated play all the muscles of the body—an important factor in attaining complete, well-rounded muscle development and control.

Each bounce may be considered as consisting of three phases—the *drop,* during which movement is completed and the body assumes the proper position for landing; and the *landing* and *take-off,* during which various body actions are coordinated to work the bed, and the lift and control necessary for recovery or the execution of the next movement are obtained. While the fundamental bounces may be thought of in this three-phased capacity for purposes of discussion, in actual execution all three phases are blended into one continuous process called the *beat.* On the pages which follow, each of the seven bounces has been divided into four phases, each illustrated separately. In studying these illustrations, it must be kept in mind that all action takes place directly above a single point on the bed; and that "traveling"—moving forward or backward from this point—is not desirable, except when specifically indicated in text or illustrations.

It is recommended that the seven fundamental bounces be taught in the order in which they are presented here, experience having shown that learning is most rapid when this procedure is followed. Throughout this instruction, the instructor should be alert for off-balance take-offs, landings which jerk or jar the body, mat burns, and other indications of faulty execution. Time consumed in learning perfect execution of the seven fundamental bounces

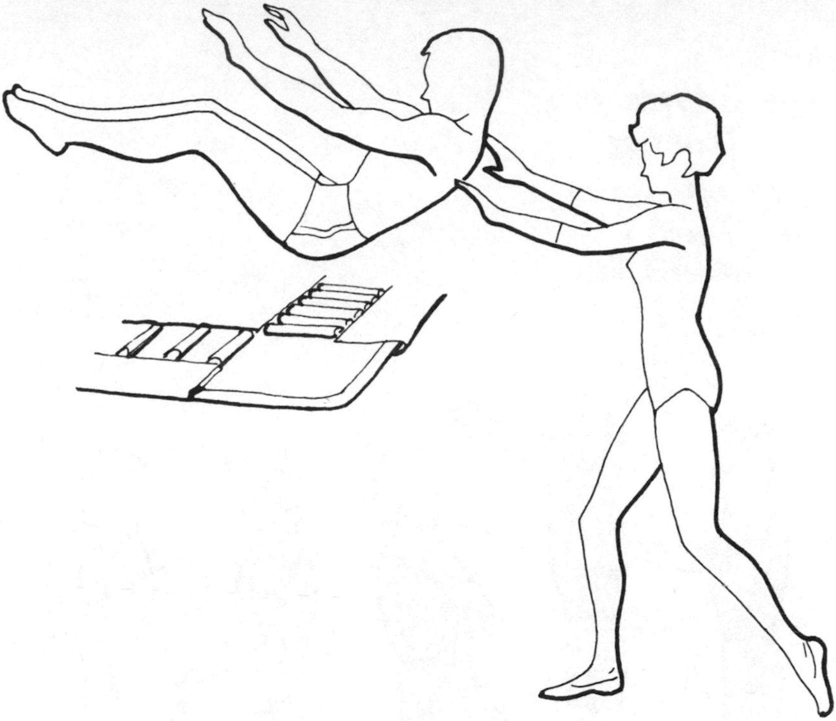

is well spent, for once the student is thoroughly grounded in these basic skills, more advanced work is approached with greater assurance, is more easily mastered, and, generally, is more perfectly performed.

FEET BOUNCE

The feet bounce is started from a standing position. The feet should be placed 12 to 15 inches apart, for stability. The arms are lifted up and to the sides, and the body raised up on the toes. The arms are then rotated and swung sharply downward, elbows flexed, and the hips and knees are bent. As the arms reach the bottom of their swing, the hips and knees are forcefully extended, and the heels brought down against the bed. As the arms again swing up, the toes are pushed down, the body is tensed,

FEET BOUNCE

(Straight Bounce)

NO. 1

(Fundamental Bounce)

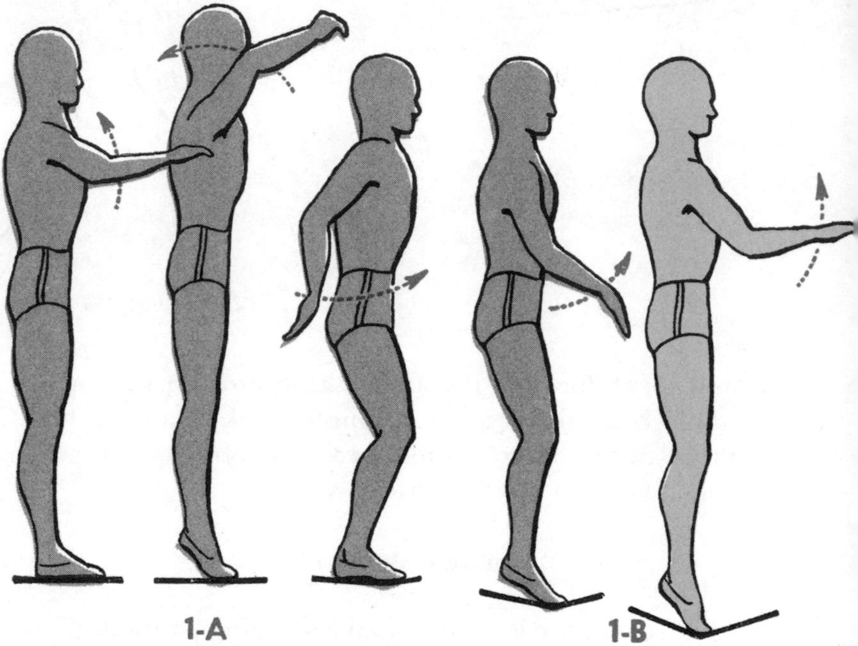

1-A

Head erect, weight on balls of feet. Look forward and *downward* at the bed. Rise on toes as arms are raised; swing arms down sharply, and flex hips and knees.

1-B

Extend hips and knees as arms swing up, extend ankles and feet to drive the bed down as far as possible. Recoil of bed launches body into air.

and the recoil of the bed thrusts the body into the air. The arms continue to swing upward, slowing in a "floating" movement as the body reaches the peak of the bounce.

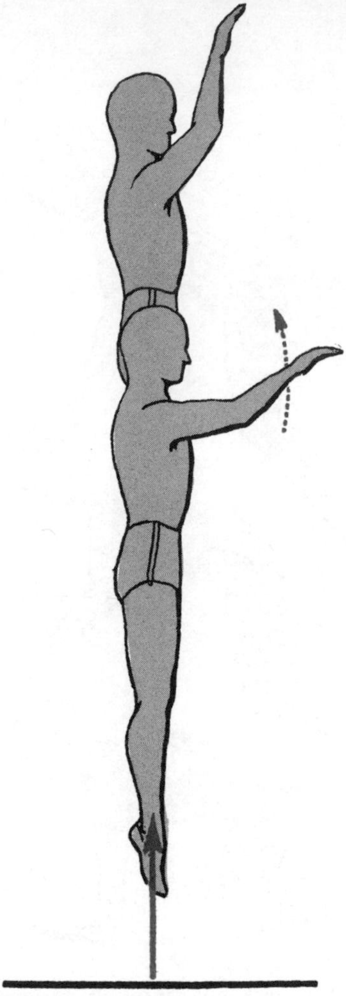

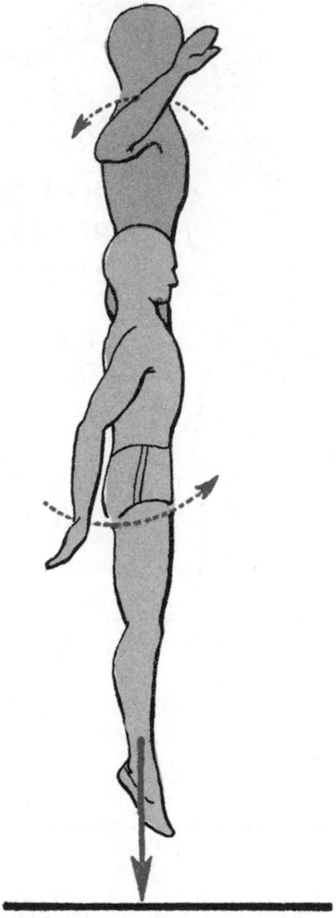

1-C

Bring feet together during ascent; keep toes pointed down. "Float" arms at top of swing; keep eyes on bed. Bring arms into position for downward swing.

1-D

Keep vision fixed on bed. As landing is made, swing arms down and through; flex, then extend, hips and knees, and swing arms up for new take-off. *Spot it!*

As the body descends, the arms are brought into position to repeat the strong downward beat on landing.

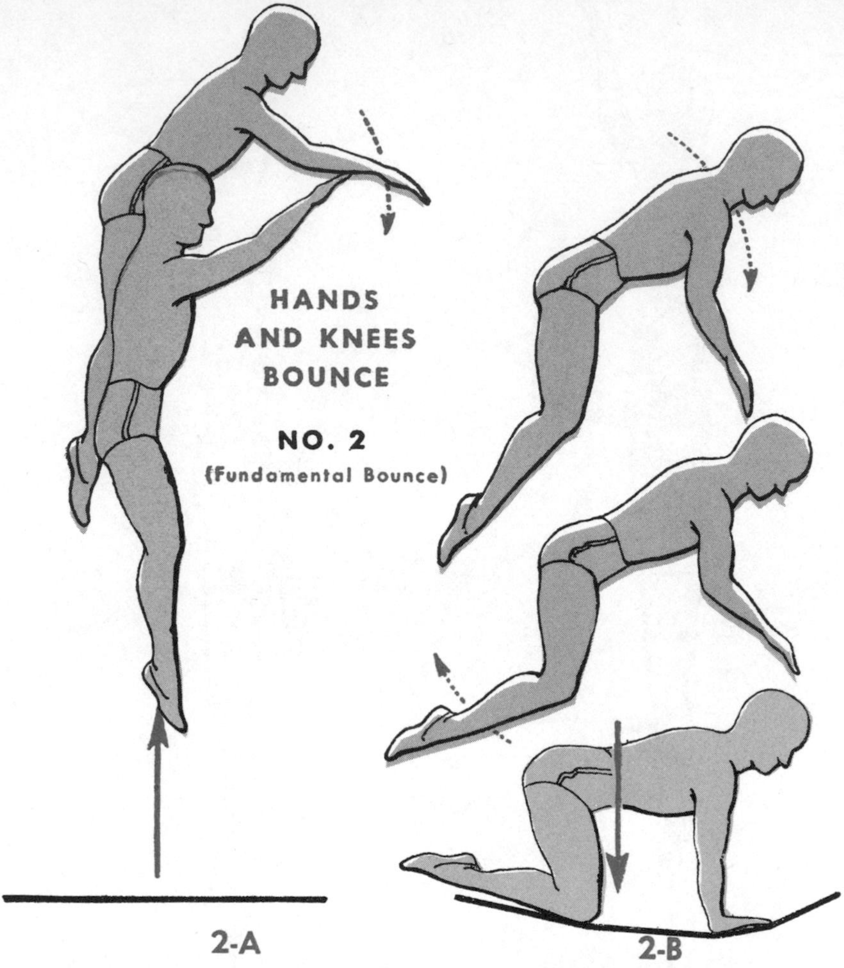

2-A

Head erect, hips back—eyes directed downward. As top of bounce is neared, bring arms forward and down, pulling head and shoulders in same direction.

2-B

Flex hips and knees, bring arms, head, and shoulders forward and down. Glance at landing spot. Land on four points—keep head up, no weight on insteps. *Spot it!*

HANDS AND KNEES BOUNCE

Hips are thrown back slightly at take-off. During the ascent the hips are allowed to rise, and the arms are brought forward and downward, carrying the head and

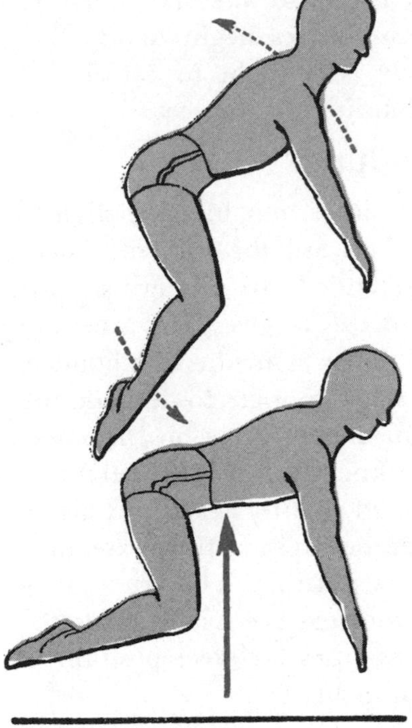

2-C

At take-off, bring arms up, throw head and shoulders back. Begin to extend hips and knees when body has cleared the bed. Keep vision fixed on bed.

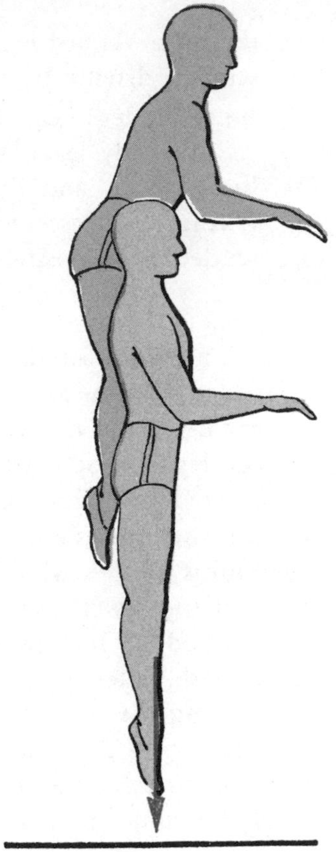

2-D

As body descends, complete the extension of hips and knees, and bring body into erect position for landing on feet. Illustration shows landing preparatory to executing break.

shoulders in the same direction. As the body descends, the head and shoulders continue forward and downward, and the hips and knees are flexed and raised. As contact is made, the back is horizontal, the arms are down, and the knees are well bent and drawn slightly forward under the hips. As bed is depressed, the arms are flexed and extended, driving the bed down still further. At the same time, the legs beat down, then up, in a rapid movement. As the body leaves the bed, the head and shoulders are brought up, and the hips and knees begin to unbend. During the descent, the body is brought to a fully extended, erect position for a landing on the feet.

KNEES BOUNCE

Take-off is similar to feet bounce, but hips are slightly flexed. As the body descends toward the bed, the knees are bent, and the feet—toes extended—are swung up until the legs are at right angles to the thighs. The arms are rotated and swung back and down as in the feet bounce, but the elbows are bent at a sharper angle to decrease the radius of the swing. The landing is made on the knees and the lower legs, with the knees taking the weight of the body. The hips must be held slightly flexed and firmly tensed. After contact is made, the hips are fully extended, driving the bed down as far as possible. The arms swing up during the take-off, and the legs are extended as the body rises. The body then assumes an erect position as the tumbler prepares to land on his feet.

SEAT-DROP

During the take-off, the head and shoulders are pulled slightly back. Arm action is identical to that described for the feet bounce. As the body begins to descend, the hips are flexed and the legs raised, and the head and shoulders move forward, reacting to the movement of the legs. The arms are brought directly down, hands behind the hips, with palms down and fingers forward. Landing is made on the hands, buttocks, and legs, with the upper part of the body erect, weight centered over the hips. There is no arm swing, and the legs are held tense, their weight helping to depress the bed. The arms are thrown high as

KNEES BOUNCE

NO. 3

Fundamental Bounce)

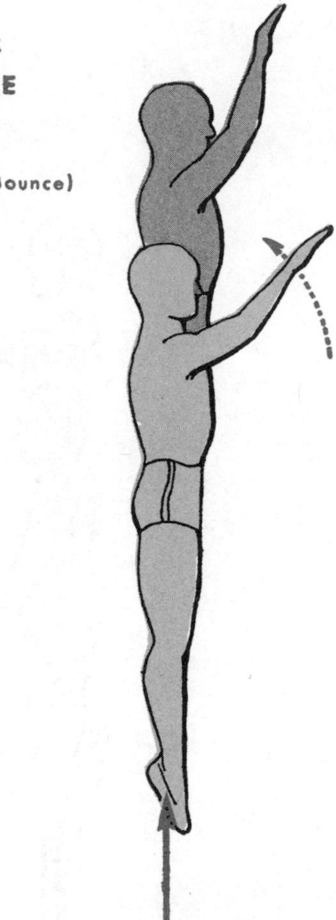

3-A

Use a low bounce for take-off. Flex hips slightly. Keep head erect, eyes forward and downward. Do not bend knees while body is rising from the bed.

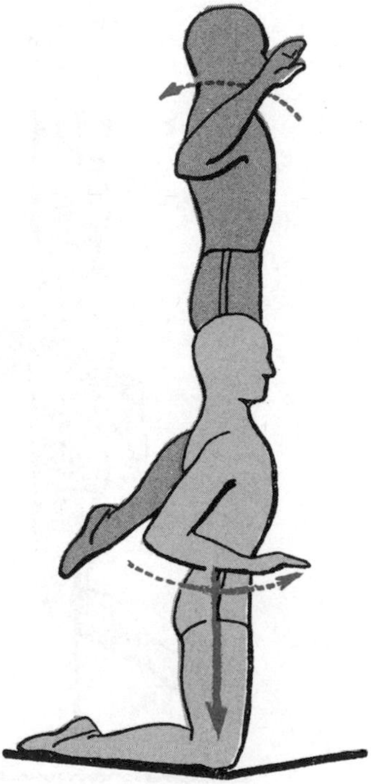

3-B

As body drops, bend knees and swing feet up. Use arm action employed in feet bounce, bending elbows sharply for short, fast swing. Extend hips after contact is made.

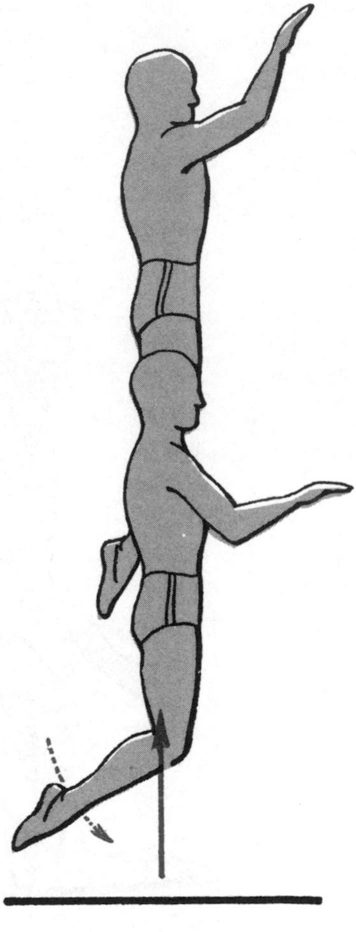

3-C

Swing arms up for lift and balance on take-off. As knees leave the bed, keep head up, and begin to unbend knees and bring feet down.

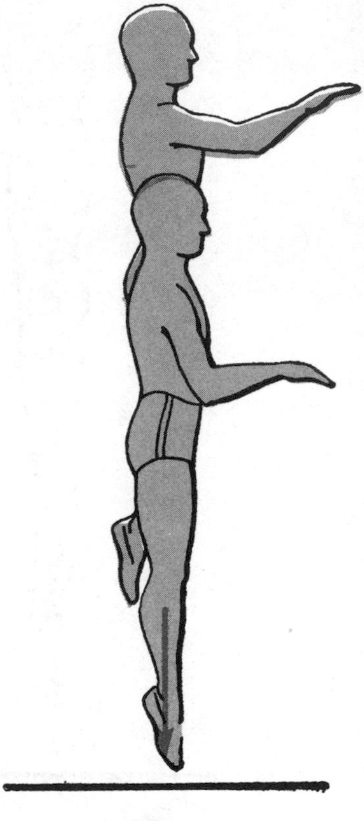

3-D

During descent, bring arms down to maintain balance and extend body into fully erect position for landing on the feet. ***Spot it!***

SEAT-DROP

NO. 4

(Fundamental Bounce)

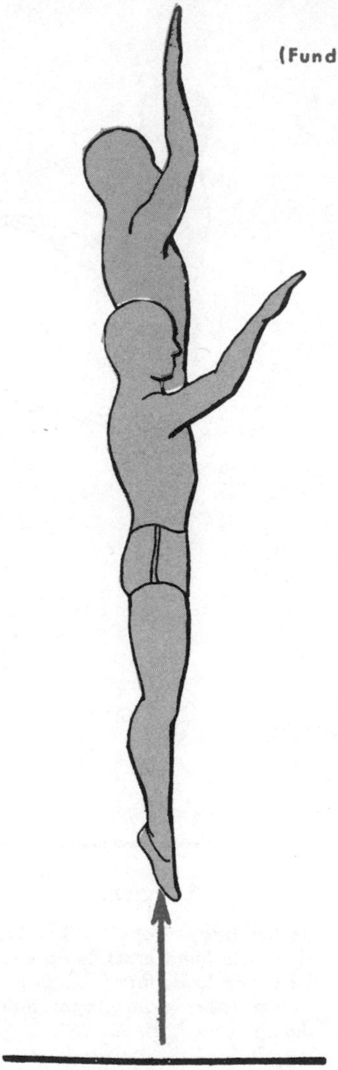

4-A

Use the same arm action on take-off as employed in the feet bounce. During the ascent, the head and shoulders are thrown back slightly, tilting body back slightly.

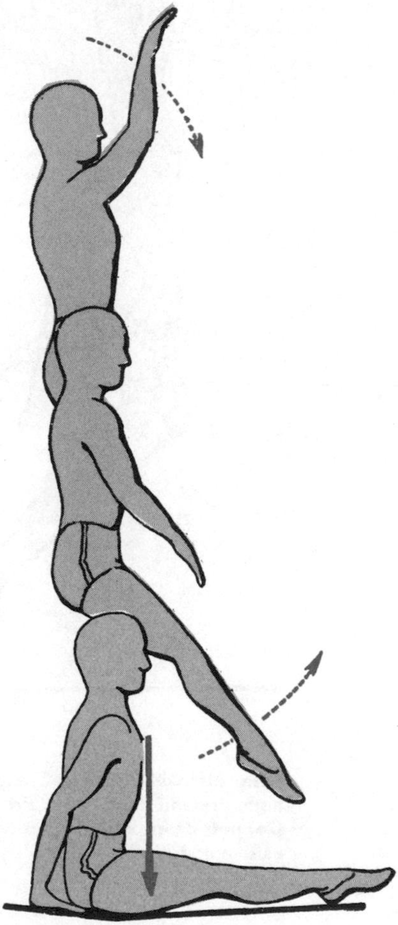

4-B

Flex hips and swing legs up. Bring arms forward and down; hands behind hips, palms down, fingers forward. Land on hands, buttocks, and hips. *Spot it!*

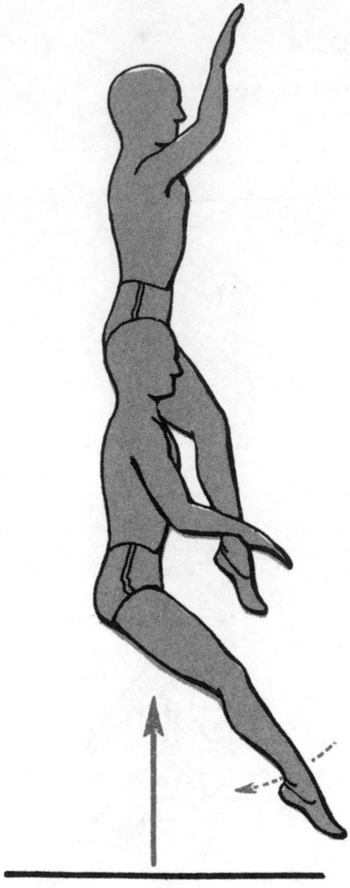

4-C

Push off with hands. Swing arms high, extend hips, and drop legs. Do not drop legs too soon—feet must not strike bed. Keep eyes forward and downward.

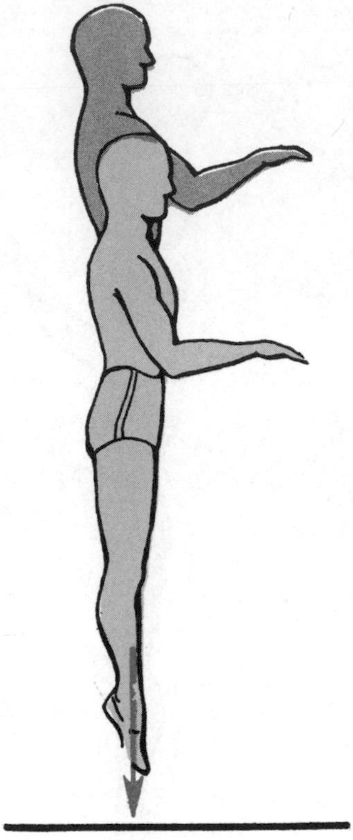

4-D

As the body drops for landing on feet, hold head erect, keep eyes on bed, and lower arms, as illustrated above, to maintain proper balance during drop.

the body rebounds from the bed. As the body ascends, the hips are extended, the legs are lowered, and the drop prior to landing is made in erect position. Landing is made on the feet.

FRONT-DROP

Hips are slightly flexed and thrust back on take-off. As the top of the bounce is neared, the arms are brought forward and downward, leading the head and shoulders. As the body starts to descend, the hips and knees are flexed, and the arms continue to pull the head and shoulders down. During the drop, the body is extended, and the legs are raised. The arms—elbows sharply bent—are raised until the elbows are almost level with the shoulders. Landing is made on eight points of contact—hands, forearms, chest, abdomen, and thighs. Keep body rigid for landing. After contact is made, the hips are slightly flexed, and the arms and thighs thrust the bed down. The hands push against the bed during the take-off, and the legs are swung down, bringing the body into position for a landing on the feet.

BACK-DROP

The arms are swung up and the hips thrust forward on take-off, causing backward rotation. The head is held well forward, chin on chest, and the eyes are focused on the end of the frame. During the descent, the hips and knees are flexed, and the knees are drawn up as the body rotates backward. The landing is made with the back parallel to the bed, body rigid. As the bed is being depressed, the arms and legs execute a quick, short extension, tending to further depress the bed. As the body rebounds, the knees are straightened, the hips are thrust up and forward, and the head and shoulders are raised. At the top of the bounce, the body is arched. The head and shoulders are pulled erect, and the legs are brought down and under the center of weight as the body is extended prior to landing.

FRONT-DROP

NO. 5

(Fundamental Bounce)

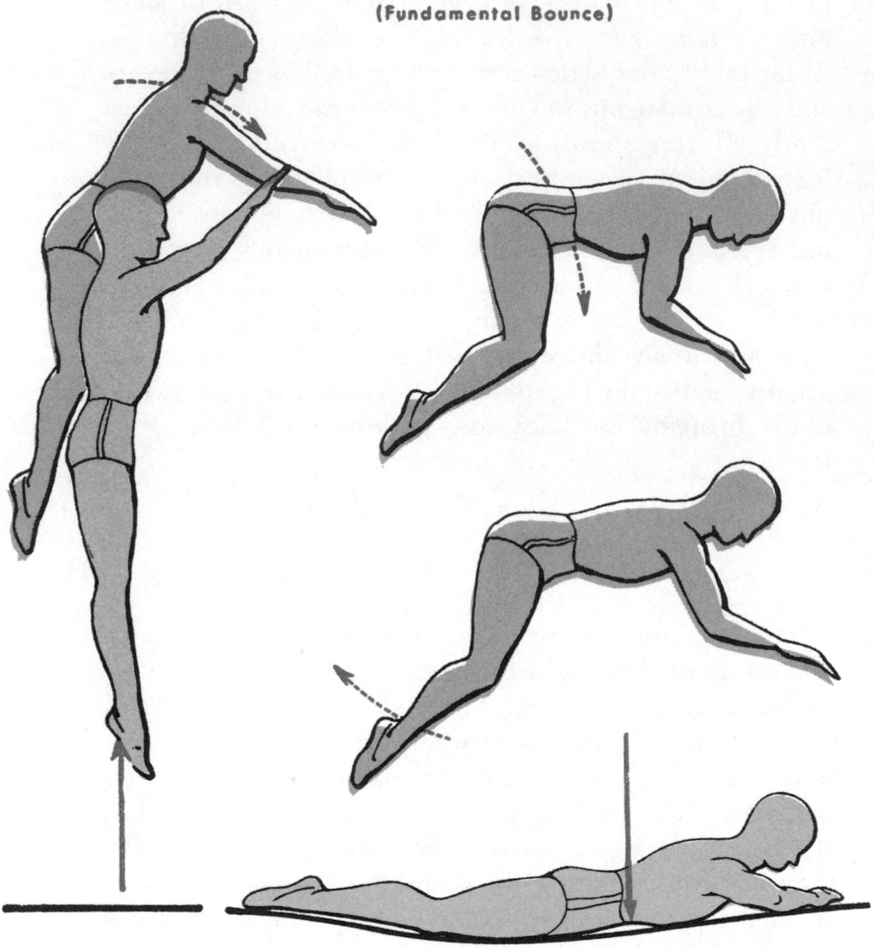

5-A

5-B

Flex hips and knees and thrust hips back at take-off. Bring arms forward and down to pull head and shoulders forward. Look down at landing spot, holding head back.

Continue forward rotation until back is horizontal. Extend legs and raise head. Keep legs low during drop. Land flat to avoid body snap. Do not land on elbows. *Spot it!*

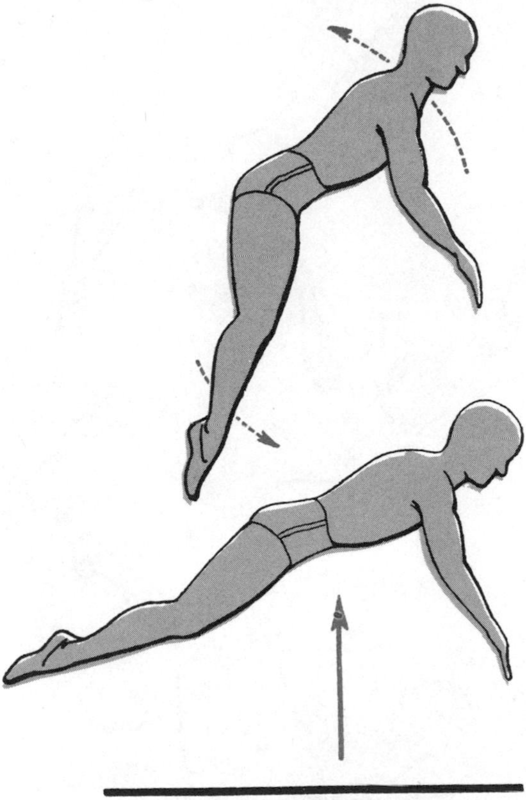

5-C

Push off strongly with hands on take-off. Raise arms, head, and shoulders. Bend hips and swing legs down. Check position with reference to landing spot.

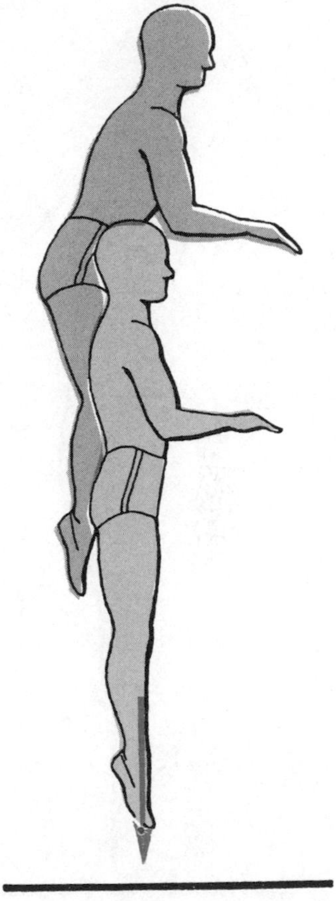

5-D

As the body drops, extend hips and straighten into erect position for landing—head up, vision fixed on bed, feet held about 15 inches apart.

BACK-DROP

NO. 6

(Fundamental Bounce)

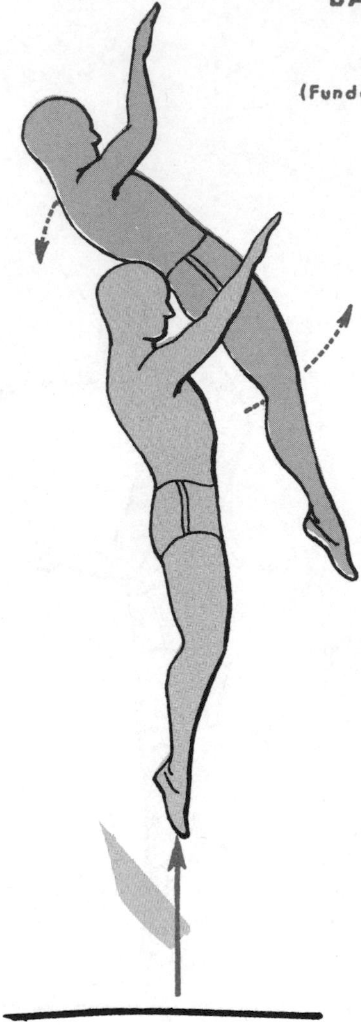

6-A

Throw arms high and thrust hips forward on take-off. Let legs swing up and shoulders drop back and down. Bend head forward, chin on chest.

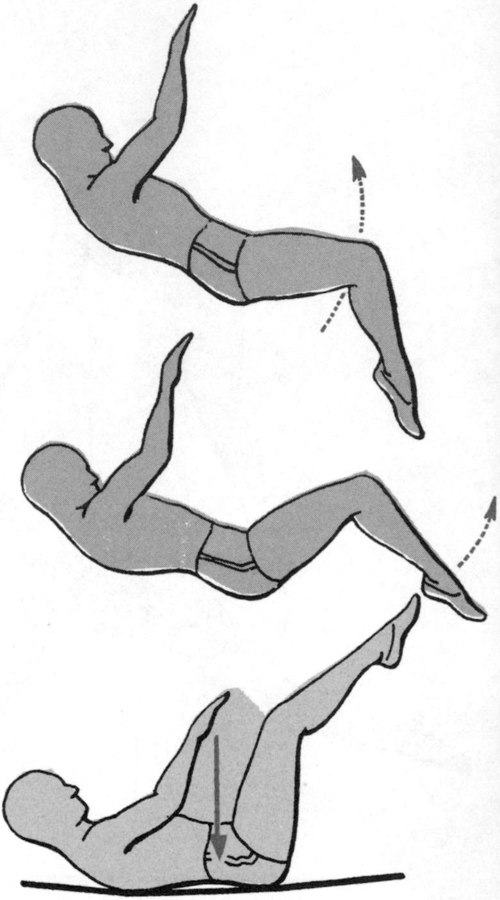

6-B

Bend hips and knees, draw knees up toward chest as body drops. Land flat on back, body rigid, head well forward, *chin on chest, eyes on end of frame. Spot it!*

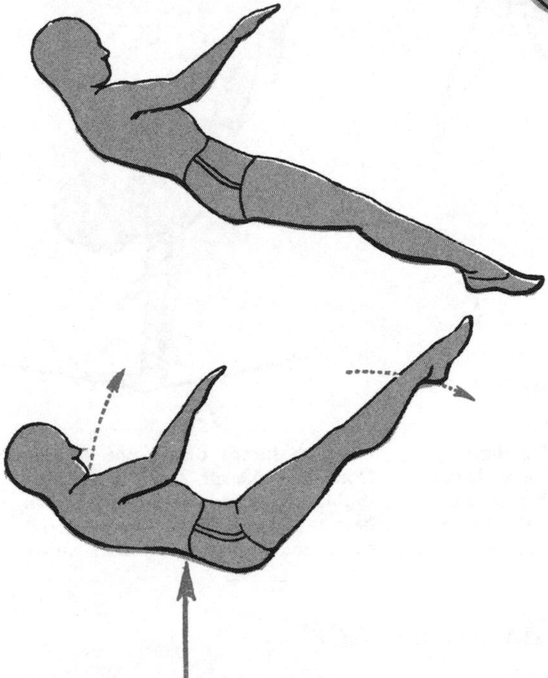

6-C

As the body rebounds from the bed, straighten the legs and bring the head and shoulders up and forward—then thrust hips up and forward. Keep *chin on chest, eyes on end of frame.*

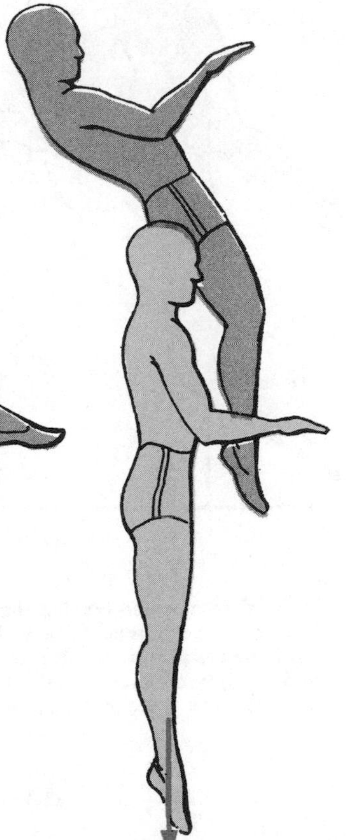

6-D

Continue hip thrust, arching body, and allow legs to swing down and under as head and shoulders rise to erect position. Straighten out for landing.

HANDS
BOUNCE
NO. 7

(Fundamental Bounce)

7-A

Take off from knees, leaning slightly forward. Keep bounce very low. Straighten legs and flex hips as feet clear bed; throw head and shoulders forward, and bring arms down.

7-B

Land on hands about one foot in front of take-off spot. Arch back slightly and allow arms and knees to flex to absorb shock. Then extend arms and legs, driving bed down.

HANDS BOUNCE

In trampoline tumbling, the hands are used mainly to afford momentary support, usually in the form of an assisting technique in low-bounce exercises involving handsprings, round-offs, and the like. When employed in the execution of single exercises, such as the "donkey kick" shown here, the take-off is made with a low bounce from the knees, with the body leaning slightly forward. The

7-C

As body rises from bed, throw head back and flex hips, bring legs down and raise the head and shoulders. Keep center of weight slightly behind hands at all times.

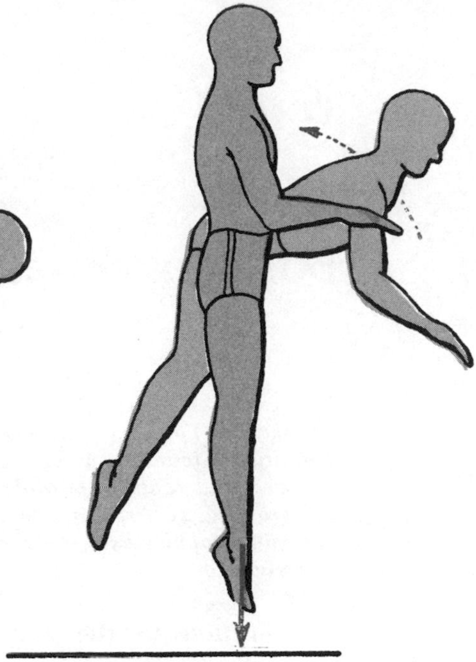

7-D

As body drops continue to bring legs down and head and shoulders upward and backward, extending as the body reaches a vertical position prior to landing.

hips are flexed and lifted upward sharply as the head and shoulders go forward and downward only, resulting in a very low bounce. As the landing is made on the hands, the knees flex, absorbing shock. The arms and knees are extended to work the bed. As the body rebounds, the head and shoulders are brought up and the legs are carried down, placing the body in position for a landing on the feet.

6

Basic Exercises

The exercises described and illustrated in this section are basic in nature. Together with easily mastered variations, they constitute a foundation for rapid progress into the more advanced exercises and routines possible in trampoline tumbling. Exercises are grouped with relation to take-off positions, and certain of the more popular exercises are illustrated as examples of correct execution.

In addition to the skillful application of previously-learned techniques, the trampoline tumbler must possess both confidence and courage to meet the challenge of new exercises. Confidence he gains from well-learned fundamentals, but courage is a personal attribute. Each new exercise represents a step forward in trampoline tumbling —and it takes real courage to venture each new step. True, the student is safeguarded from danger by manual assistance, and well-learned fundamentals have prepared him for each step forward. Nevertheless, the fact remains that he is essentially "on his own". In effect, he "pioneers" each exercise. If any doubt exists in the reader's mind as to the courage required and displayed in trampoline tumbling, watch, for instance, a student as he first performs a bent dive. Note the set, determined expression, the tenseness of the entire body—usually much too tense. Summoning all his courage, the individual throws himself into the exercise almost blindly. Then note the half-surprised look of satisfaction when the landing is made on the back, followed by the rebound to the feet. The landing and rebound were made almost instinctively, because the fundamental skills involved were properly learned. But it took courage—courage and confidence—to "get started" and put those skills to use. Once achieved, the "strange, new exercise" becomes no longer strange, but merely a "new exercise"—and satisfaction is all the greater for the knowledge that courage was required to attempt it.

One further word about courage. Without due regard for rules, courage becomes foolhardiness. The student must learn that, in trampoline tumbling, skipping steps of progressive learning is foolhardy. The tumbler who attempts exercises for which he is unprepared subjects himself needlessly to danger—an indication not of courage, but of stupidity. Progress is not only safer but faster for the student who learns his fundamentals well. He is in a position to make his training work for him, and is not faced with the necessity of "unlearning" improper techniques, or relearning some skill which he should have mastered previously.

SWIVEL HIPS

The half twist may be executed either to right or left, according to which seems more natural. Many students are able, and should be encouraged, to do it either way. At take-off the hands push off the bed sharply and are lifted, in full extension, forward and upward as the body rises. The legs are swung downward in pendulum fashion, straight and together with toes pointed, at the same speed the arms are swung upward. As the arms near the top of their reach, the body starts twisting with the hips leading,

as shown in the illustration above. When the body is fully extended it is halfway through the half twist. The arms are continued through their circular sweep to complete the twist. Likewise, the legs continue their pendulum swing to the seat-drop landing. In this exercise it is important that the head does not lead the twist but stays squarely aligned with the shoulders throughout the entire stunt.

HALF TURNTABLE

Take-off is made in front-drop position. The thighs

HALF TURNTABLE
(or Bluch)
NO. 2
(Basic Exercise)

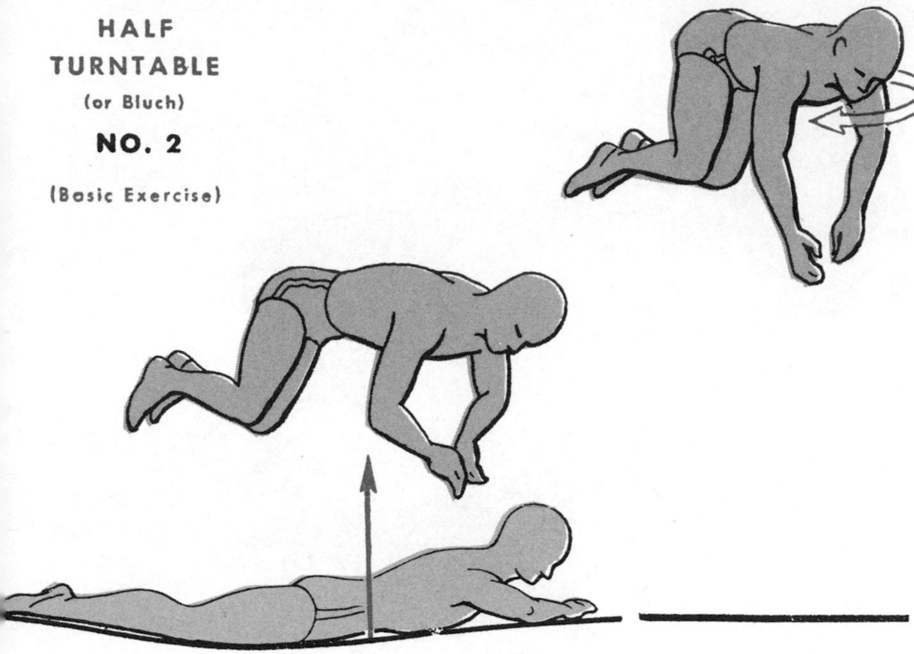

2-A

Push off forcefully. Use hands to start body in spin to the right. Throw head and shoulders in direction of spin. Draw knees under body.

2-B

Keep arms down and knees and hips well flexed to bring body-mass close to center of rotation. Keep head and shoulders low, eyes on bed.

push directly down against the bed, and the hands exert a strong push down and to the left, starting the body spinning to the right. The head and shoulders are thrown to the right, contributing to the spin. (Half side-spin may be made to right or left—illustration shows spin to right.) As the body clears the bed, the hips and knees are flexed, and the knees are drawn down and forward. Arms are allowed to hang in a semi-flexed position. The head and shoulders are kept low, and the back remains parallel to the bed during the spin. As the body drops and the half

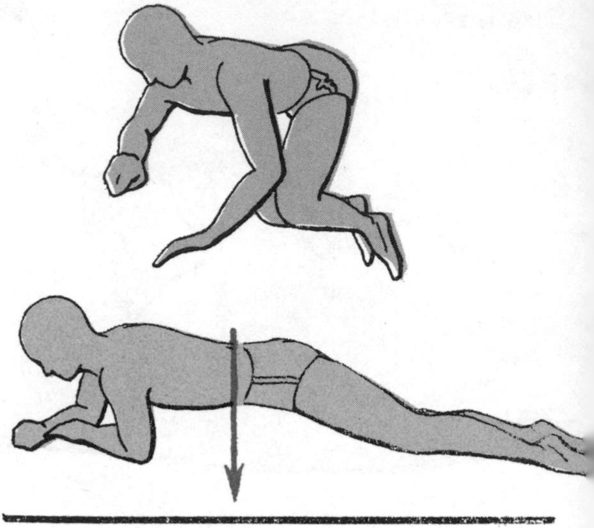

2-C

Hold legs and feet together. Keep back parallel to surface of bed throughout spin. Arms remain down in semi-flexed position.

2-D

When half spin is almost complete, extend hips and knees to raise legs and halt spin. Raise head and arms —elbows bent—for landing.

spin nears completion, the hips and knees are extended, raising the legs, the arms are flexed and raised, and the head is brought up before the landing is made in front-drop position.

FRONT SOMERSAULT–(Knees to Seat)

Hips are flexed slightly and thrust back for take-off. The

FRONT SOMERSAULT

KNEES TO SEAT

NO. 3

(Basic Exercise)

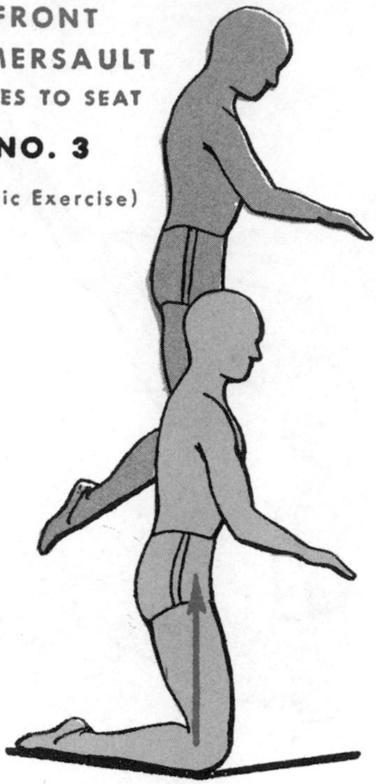

3-A

Thrust hips back for take-off. Push down with feet as body rises from bed, and throw head and shoulders forward to start rotation.

3-B

Flex hips and knees, grasp legs above ankles, and pull head and shoulders forward toward knees into tight tuck. Keep head bent forward.

feet exert a slight push-off as the body rises, and the head and shoulders are thrown forward. The hips and knees are tightly flexed, and—as the body tips forward—the legs are grasped just above the ankles and the head and shoulders are pulled forward toward the knees. Due to the low height of bounce, this tucking action must be rapid and forceful to effect rapid rotation. The tuck is held until

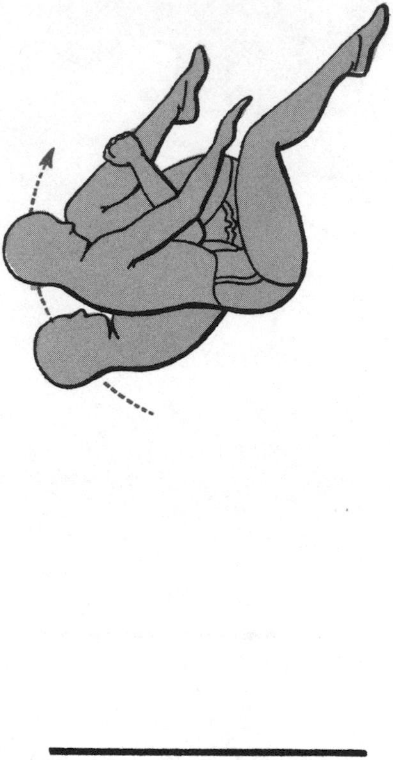

3-C

Tuck must be tight and fast to achieve rapid rotation. Hold tuck until somersault is three-fourths completed, then straighten legs, keeping hips flexed.

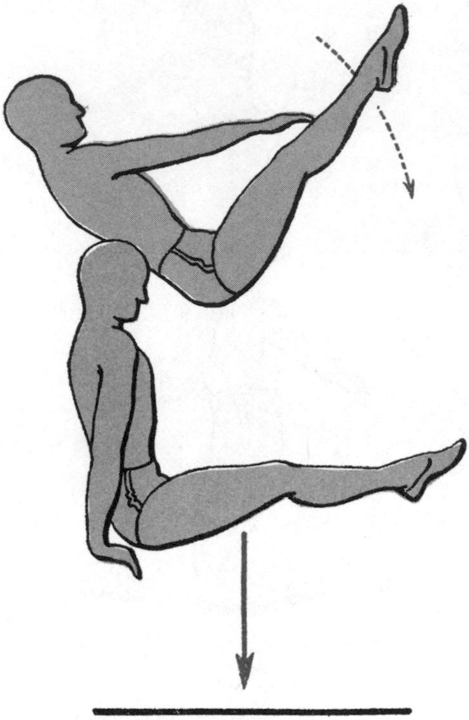

3-D

Raise head and complete rotation in semi-pike position. Bring arms down and back and hold body rigid for seat-drop landing.

the somersault is three-fourths completed. As the tuck is broken, the legs are straightened but the hips remain flexed, placing the body in a semi-pike position. The head is raised as the upper part of the body rotates to an erect position, and the arms are brought down and back into position the body as the seat-drop landing is made.

FRONT TURNOVER

HANDS AND KNEES TO FEET

NO. 4

(Basic Exercise)

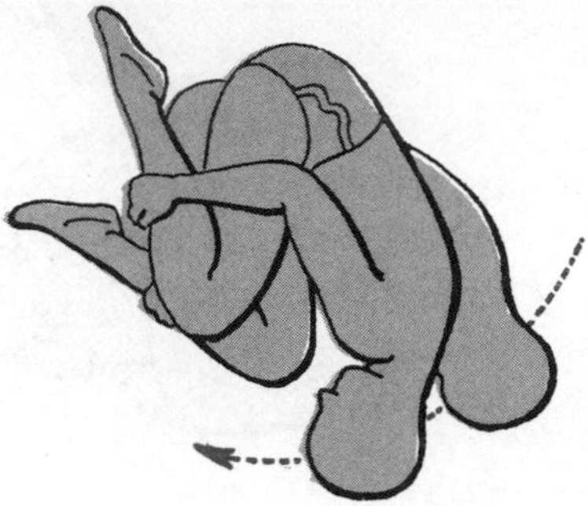

4-A

Thrust hips up on take-off. As body leaves bed, push off with feet. Throw head forward and swing arms forward to start rotation.

4-B

As body rises, bring head and shoulders forward, flex hips and knees, grasp legs, and assume tight tuck position.

FRONT TURNOVER—(Hands and Knees to Feet)

The hips are thrust high at take-off to start forward rotation. During the ascent, the hips and knees are fully flexed, the legs are grasped below the knees, and the chest and shoulders are pulled forward against the thighs in a

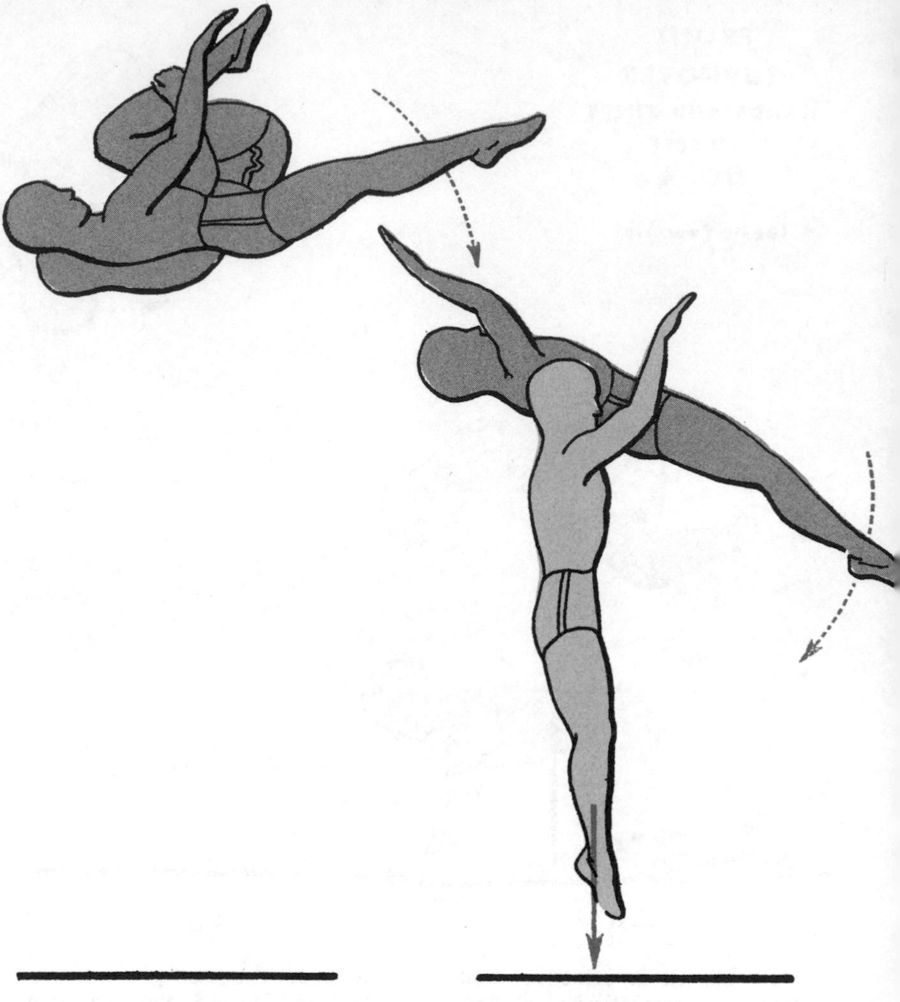

4-C

Come out when somersault is about three-fourths completed. Raise head and arms, unbend hips, and straighten legs to check rotation.

4-D

During descent, bring legs down under center of weight and extend body in fully erect position for landing on the feet.

tight tuck. The head should be bent well forward after take-off, but not so quickly as to result in a low bounce. When the somersault is about two-thirds completed, the body is extended and the arms are raised to check rotation. As the legs drop down, the hips are unflexed, and the head and shoulders swing up toward a vertical position. As the head and shoulders approach an erect position, the arms are brought up, the legs are carried down and under the center of weight, and the body is brought to the proper position for a well-balanced landing on the feet.

FRONT SOMERSAULT—(Feet to Feet)

At the take-off, the hips are thrust back and the arms swung forward and down to start forward rotation. As the body rises, the head and shoulders are thrown forward and the hips and knees are flexed. The legs are grasped between knees and ankles, the upper part of the body is pulled forward against the thighs, and the heels are pulled tight against the buttocks. The kick-out is made when the somersault is about three-fourths completed. The head is raised, the arms are extended and raised, and the body is straightened to slow rotation. The head and shoulders rise and the legs swing down as the body assumes an erect position. The feet should be held close together until just before contact with the bed—then they are separated to insure stability on landing. (see page 98 for progressive steps in learning.)

BARANI

The barani is a forward somersault with a half twist in which the head is not ducked forward and the eyes are focused on the bed throughout the entire stunt. In the take-off the hips are thrust back as for a piked somersault, with arms wide apart. The head and shoulders rotate forward and the hips flex as they rise. As the head-down position is approached the left arm sweeps across in front of the legs to the right, initiating twist in upper body. Now the hips are extended vigorously, straightening the body, pulling the hips into the twist already initiated by

FRONT SOMERSAULT

FEET TO FEET

NO. 5

(Basic Exercise)

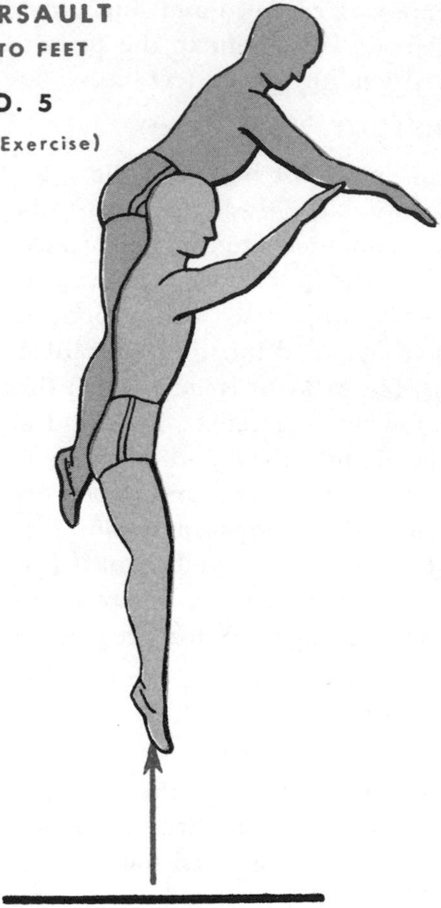

5-A

Thrust hips back on take-off. Do not dive forward—as body rises, flex hips and swing arms forward and down, starting forward rotation.

5-B

Throw head and shoulders forward as body ascends. Flex hips and knees, grasp shins, and pull chest and shoulders forward into tuck.

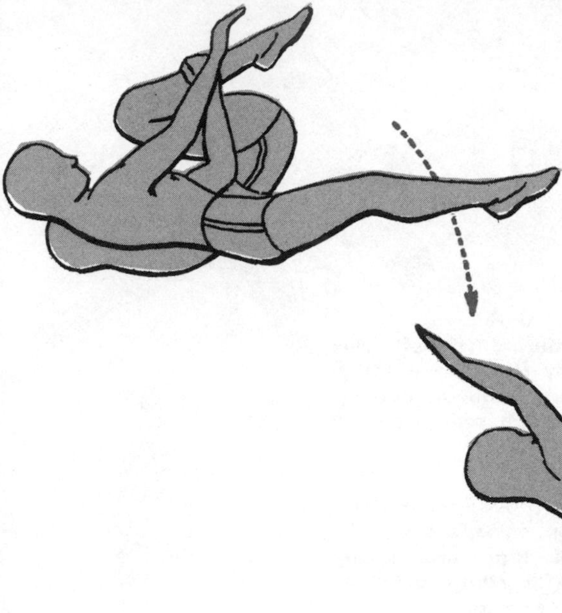

5-C

When somersault is three-fourths completed, raise head, bring arms up and extend body to retard rotation. Keep legs together in come-out.

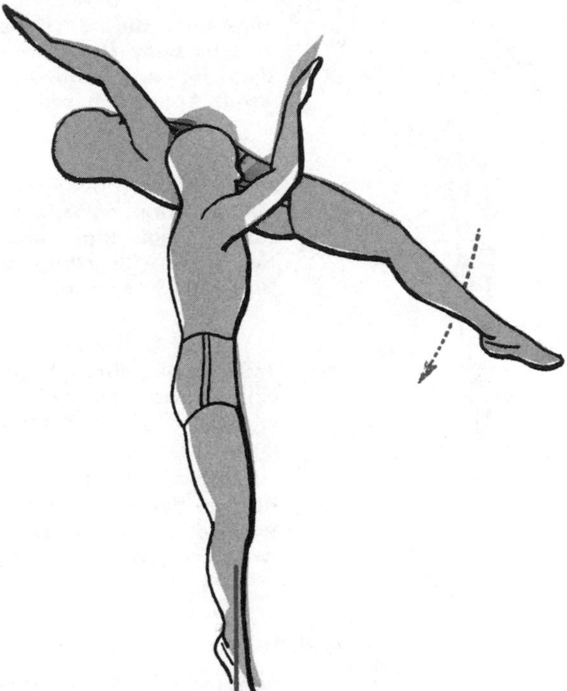

5-D

Swing arms up and bring feet under center of weight as body rotates to erect position. Hold feet about 15 inches apart for stable landing.

BARANI
NO. 6
(Basic Exercise)

6-A
Hips back during take-off. Flex hips as body rises. Bring shoulders forward without ducking head. Arms high and wide.

6-B
As body nears head-down position left arm sweeps across in front of legs. Right arm is carried back with elbow bending. Hips start to extend.

6-C
Body passes through this fully extended position with both arms in front of chest, elbows in.

6-D
Hips are flexed and arms brought forward and sideward to check twist. Feet are brought down for landing.

the shoulders, and bringing the right arm to front of chest. As the twist nears completion, the arms are extended to the front and the hips are flexed to check rotations for the landing. (See page 90 for steps in learning.)

BACKOVER—(Back-Drop to Feet)

The legs are held high during the take-off, swinging over and back as the body rises. The head is held well forward until sufficient height for easy execution of the

BACKOVER

BACK-DROP TO FEET

NO. 7

(Basic Exercise)

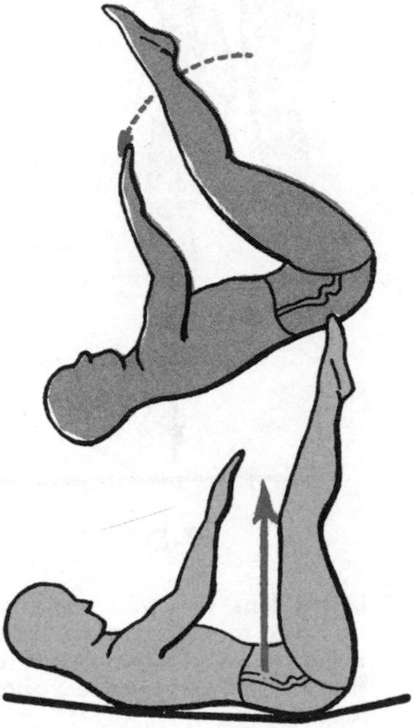

7-A

Hold legs high at take-off. Swing legs back and over as body rises, starting backward rotation. Keep head well forward while gaining height.

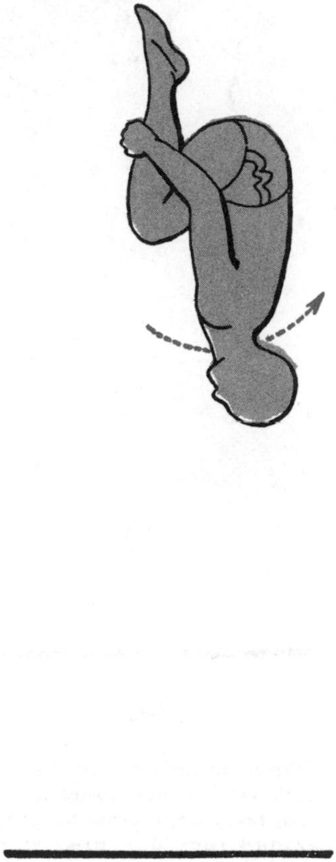

7-B

Throw head back sharply. Flex hips and knees, grasp legs and pull them up and over toward chest. Low bounce necessitates fast, tight tuck.

backover is gained. Then the head is thrown back forcefully, the hips and knees are tightly flexed, and the arms

7-C

Keep head back and hold tuck until backover is almost completed. Then —as body approaches horizontal— extend legs and arms to slow rotation.

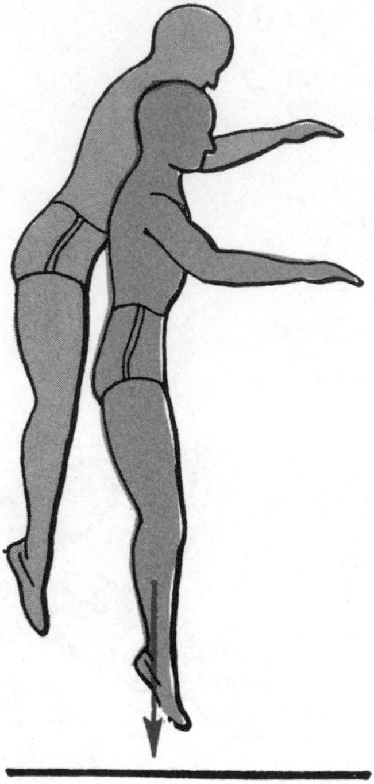

7-D

Unflex hips and raise upper part of body to erect position as legs swing down. Center weight over feet as body is extended prior to landing.

pull the legs over toward the chest. Here—as in the case of the backward somersault from seat-drop position—the low bounce necessitates a tight, fast tuck. The tuck is held until the backover is almost completed. Then—as the head and shoulders swing up and the body approaches a horizontal position—the arms are extended and raised and the legs are straightened, retarding rotation. As the

BACK SOMERSAULT
SEAT TO FEET
NO. 8
(Basic Exercise)

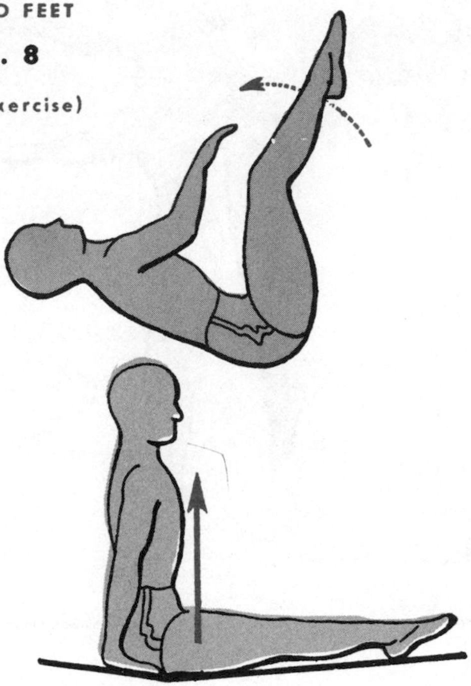

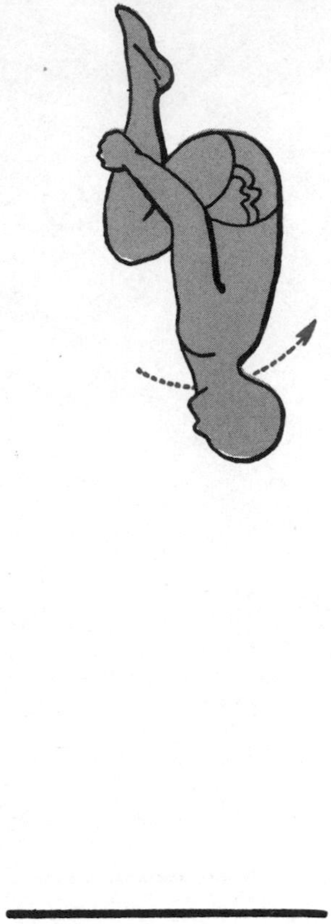

8-A
Lean back slightly on take-off. Raise arms and throw head back. Flex hips and raise legs as head and shoulders drop down and backward.

8-B
Flex hips and knees tightly. Grasp legs below knees, and pull knees up and over toward chest. Keep head back; look for landing spot.

legs swing down, the hips are unflexed and the head and shoulders are raised to an erect position as the body drops feet-first for the landing.

BACK SOMERSAULT—(Seat to Feet)

The upper part of the body is inclined slightly back-

8-C

Hold tight tuck until somersault is three-fourths completed. Break tuck, raising arms and straightening legs to check rotation.

8-D

Allow legs to drop and head and shoulders to rise, then extend the body in erect position preparatory to landing on the feet.

ward at the take-off. As the body begins to rise, the arms are raised, and the head is bent sharply back, leading the head and shoulders down as the legs swing up. The hips and knees are fully flexed, and the hands grasp the legs below the knees, pulling the legs up and over toward the chest in a tight, fast tuck. As the body rotates through the head-down position, the eyes pick up the landing spot on the bed. The tuck is broken when the somersault is three-fourths completed—the arms are raised and the legs straightened to check rotation. As the come-out is made, the legs drop, the head and shoulders swing up, and the body is extended in erect position—head up, feet apart, arms controlling balance—in preparation for a landing on the feet.

BACKOVER—(Feet to Hands and Knees)

At take-off, the hips are thrust well forward to induce backward rotation as the body leaves the bed. During the ascent, the head and shoulders are thrown back and the legs are swung up and back. The hips and knees are flexed, but the body is not tucked. It remains "frozen" in a semi-flexed position. The head is held well back, and —as the body rotates through the head-down position— the eyes spot the landing point. As the head swings up and the body approaches a horizontal position, the body position is adjusted for the landing. During the drop, the hips and knees are more fully flexed. The arms are extended down, the knees are brought forward under the hips, and the eyes are focused on the end of the frame. The body is held rigid in this position for the landing on hands and knees.

BACK SOMERSAULT—(Feet to Feet)

The body is slightly arched as the hips are thrust forward during the take-off. As the body leaves the bed, the legs are flexed and swung up, and the head and shoulders are thrown back. The hips and knees are tightly flexed, and the legs are grasped between ankles and knees and pulled over toward the chest in a tight tuck. As in all backward somersaults, the eyes are focused on the landing spot when the bed comes into view, allowing the tumbler to adjust timing. The tuck is held until the somersault is three-fourths completed, then the arms and legs are ex-

BACKOVER

FEET TO HANDS AND KNEES

NO. 9

(Basic Exercise)

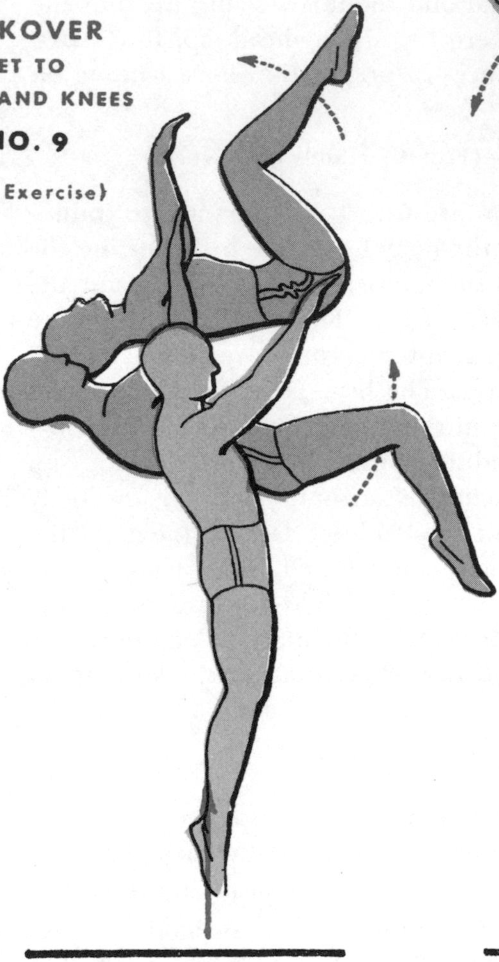

9-A

Thrust hips forward on take-off. Throw head and shoulders back, flex hips and knees partially, as illustrated. Do not tuck.

9-B

Keep head thrown back. As body reaches head-down position, locate landing spot when bed comes into view to gauge come-out.

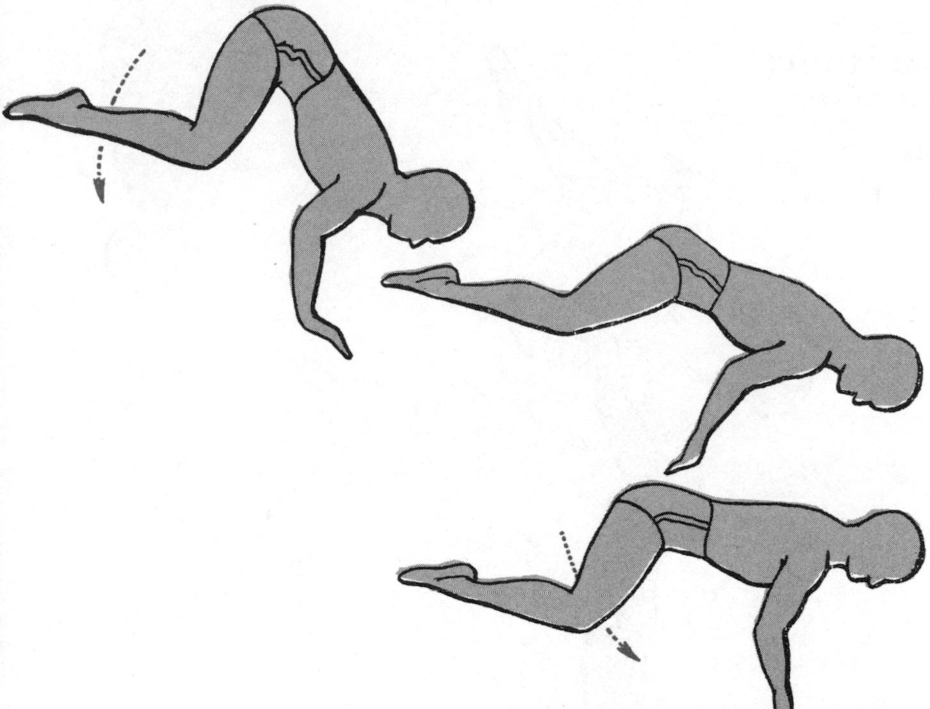

9-C

Stay "frozen" in flexed position assumed in 9-A as body approaches a face-down horizontal position. Keep eyes focused on landing-spot.

9-D

As body drops, flex hips and knees more fully, and extend arms toward bed. Pull knees forward under hips and raise head prior to landing.

BACK SOMERSAULT
FEET TO FEET

NO. 10
(Basic Exercise)

10-A

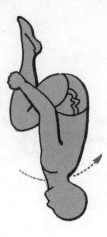

Swing arms up and thrust hips forward on take-off. Tuck legs up sharply, flexing hips and knees. Throw head and shoulders back.

10-B

Grasp legs between ankles and knees, and pull legs up toward chest in tuck position. Keep head back and pick out landing spot.

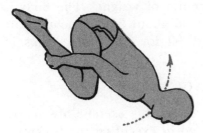

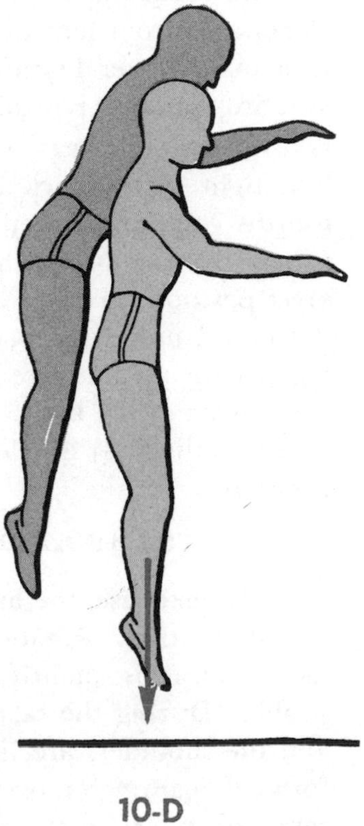

10-C

Keep eyes on landing spot. Hold tuck until somersault is three-fourths completed—then extend arms and legs to check rotation.

10-D

Raise head and shoulders to erect position. Swing legs down and under center of weight. Separate feet prior to landing.

tended to check rotation. As the body drops, the head and shoulders rise to an erect position and the legs are brought down under the center of weight. The body is extended and the feet are held about fifteen inches apart for the landing. (See page 99 for progressive steps in learning.)

BACK SOMERSAULT—(Feet to Seat)

The take-off and tuck used in this exercise are almost identical with those employed in executing the backward somersault from feet to feet. However, more rapid rotation or a higher bounce must be attained to make the seat-drop landing possible. The hips are thrust forward at take-off, and the legs pulled over toward the chest in a fast, tight tuck. Tuck is held until somersault is three-fourths completed, then the arms and legs are extended to retard rotation. As the head and shoulders rise toward erect position, the hips are flexed and the legs are swung down and under the body. Rotation is completed as the legs swing up and are extended at right angles to the upper part of the body. The arms are brought down and back and the body is held rigid for the landing in seat-drop position.

TRAMPOLINE BACK—(Loose Layout)

In this exercise, the backward somersault is executed in layout position. Rotation is slower than when a tuck is used, and, consequently, a moderately high bounce is desirable. During the take-off, the hips are rocked forward and the shoulders are thrust back. Hip action imparts a forward "gaining" movement to the body as it rises, counteracting travel to the rear. During the ascent, the hips rise up and forward and the head and shoulders drop as the body revolves in a loose layout position. The head is thrown well back, and—as the body assumes a head-down

BACK SOMERSAULT

FEET TO SEAT

NO. 11

(Basic Exercise)

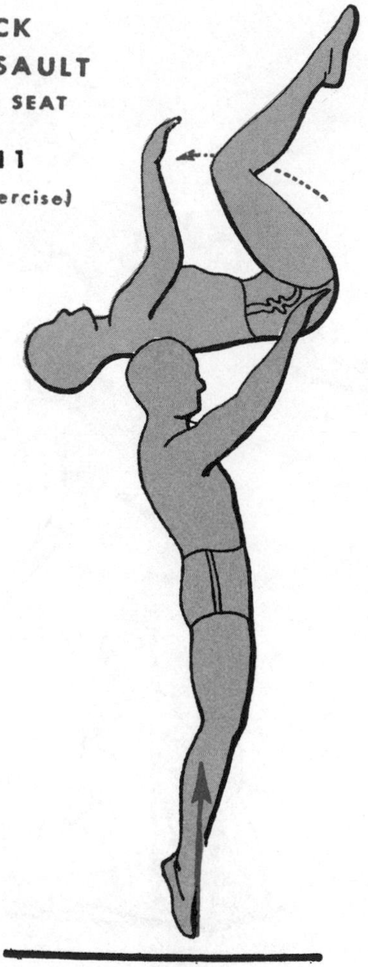

11-A

Thrust hips forward on take-off to start backward rotation. Flex hips and knees and raise legs. Throw head and shoulders back.

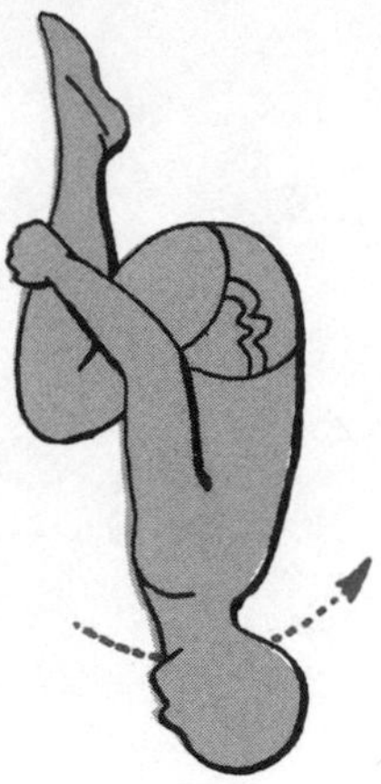

11-B

Grasp legs and pull them over toward chest. Tuck must be tight and fast. Keep head well back; look for landing spot.

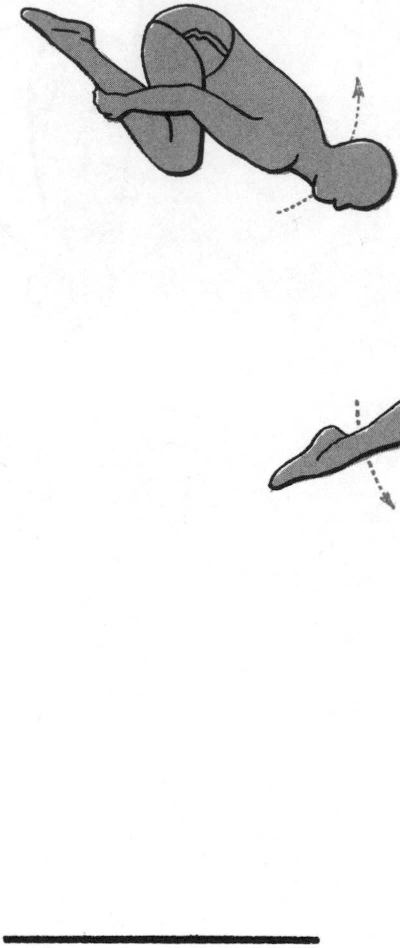

11-C

Break tuck when body reaches face-down horizontal position. Raise arms and straighten legs to slow rotation. Keep hips and knees slightly flexed.

11-D

Swing legs down and under body as head and shoulders rise. Bring arms down and back, and extend legs in seat-drop position.

TRAMPOLINE BACK

(Loose Layout Back Somersault)

FEET TO FEET

NO. 12

(Basic Exercise)

12-A

Throw shoulders back and rock hips forward during take-off. Hips come up and forward as shoulders drop. Throw head well back to aid rotation.

12-B

Hold body in loose layout position—head back, body arched, knees slightly flexed. Keep arms low and to the sides to maintain balance.

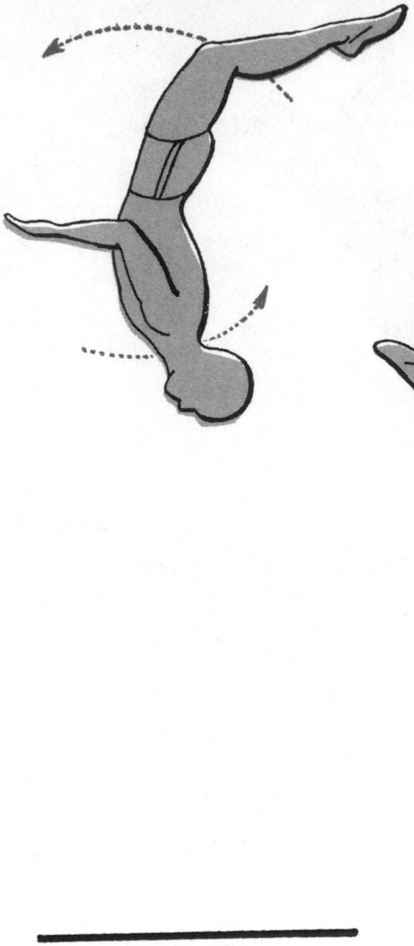

12-C

Look at landing spot as bed comes into view. Hold loose layout position, head well back, until somersault is almost completed.

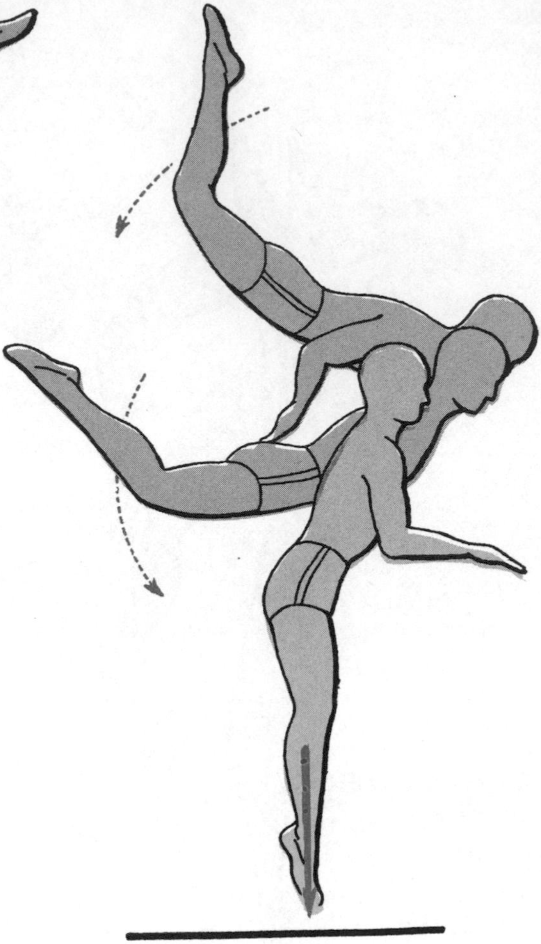

12-D

Raise head and swing legs down and under center of weight as body drops toward bed. Keep feet well apart for stable landing.

position—the eyes locate the landing spot on the bed. The body remains in layout position, back arched, until rotation is almost complete. Then the head is raised, the hips are flexed, and the legs are swung under the center of weight into position for the landing.

Feet Bounce with Half Twist—The twist is initiated as the arms reach the highest point in the upward swing which accompanies the take-off. To twist to the left, the right arm is brought downward and across the chest to the left. It is then carried away from the body, elbow bent, to the right. Coordinated with this second movement of the right arm, the left arm is brought downward and backward, elbow bent and leading. Both arms are then raised simultaneously into position for the downward swing which accompanies the landing. As the exercise is begun, the head is held erect, eyes focused on the end of the frame. When one-quarter twist has been completed, the head is turned quickly to the left, and the eyes are focused on the opposite end of the frame. Action of head and arms is reversed for twist to the right.

Feet Bounce with Full Twist—Action is similar to that employed in the execution of a half twist. For a left twist, the right arm is swung across the chest to the left and upward past the left shoulder. This rotates the body one-half turn. The right arm then is swung to the right and downward, and the left arm is swung downward and backward, completing the full twist. Arms are then raised for landing, as above. After one-quarter of the twist has been completed, the head is turned sharply to the left until the eyes pick up the original focal point on the end of the frame.

Bent Dive—The bent dive consists of a forward three-quarter somersault to a landing in the back-drop position. Take-off is made with the hips slightly flexed and to the rear of a vertical line passing through the head and feet. Legs are carried high, the hips lifted upward, and the head brought down as the body assumes a relaxed, semi-tuck position. Head is held face down until it is about three feet above the bed, then the head is quickly ducked under and the hips come down for a flat back-drop landing. Once mastered, the bent-dive may also be done in full tuck, pike, or layout position.

Forward Somersault—The following progression is recommended for learning the forward somersault:

a. Forward turnover from hands and knees take-off to back-drop or seat-drop.

b. Bent dive from knee take-off.

c. Somersault from knee take-off to seat-drop.

d. Bent dive from feet take-off.

e. Somersault from feet take-off to seat drop.

f. Somersault from knee take-off to feet, with tuck.

g. Somersault from feet take-off to feet.

Forward One-and-a-Quarter Somersault—This exercise combines the forward somersault and the front drop. The tuck is held until the somersault is slightly overturned, then a come-out is made to a semi-tucked position, the body assumes a horizontal position, and is finally extended for a front-drop landing.

Half Back (Backover to Front-Drop)—This exercise is performed in full arch-out position. At take-off, the hips are rocked forward, which results in a slight forward *gaining* movement, necessary to counteract travel to the rear.

The arms, head, and shoulders lead backward and over. The knees and hips are not flexed during rotation—the body is allowed to rotate into horizontal position for a front-drop landing.

Backward Somersault—The following progression for learning the backward somersault is recommended:

a. Backover from back-drop take-off to hands and knees.

b. Backover from back-drop take-off to feet.

c. Backover from feet take-off to hands and knees.

d. Backover from feet take-off to feet and hands.

e. Backward somersault from feet take-off to feet.

Backward One-and-a-Quarter Somersault—In this exercise, a backward somersault is overturned to a back-drop landing. After the completion of one full turn, the tuck is broken and rotation is checked by a loose kick-out, legs and trunk are aligned in horizontal position, and a regular back-drop landing is made. Some forward gain is required at take-off, and the landing must be perfect to avoid body snap. Many instructors teach a backward somersault to seat-drop as a preliminary to this exercise.

Barani—The following progression is recommended:

a. Round-off from knees take-off to knees, using hands and arms for support. Hips are flexed as a forward turnover is executed from a knees take-off; the knees remain flexed, and the hands are placed on the bed. The hips are unflexed as the body continues to a handstand position, at which point the twist is initiated. The knees are extended and the hands leave the bed as the twist is made. The hips are flexed as the legs come down, then extended as the body assumes a vertical position and the knees are flexed for the landing.

b. Round-off from knees take-off to feet, using hands and arms for support.

c. Round-off from knees take-off to knees, without support.

d. Round-off from knees take-off to feet, without support.

e. Barani (round-off from feet take-off to feet, without support).

BACK SOMERSAULT—(Free Position)

This somersault could well be called "Tramp Back" as it is specifically used only in trampolining. It should be learned by all students who consider themselves ready to organize somersaulting routines. It is a skill which is most practical to use between other more complicated stunts, especially those which begin or end with too little time to adjust for the more precise timing of the tuck, pike, or layout balance. In other words, the "free back" works "into and out of" other bounces more easily and safely.

As shown in the illustration (above OR below) the head is not thrown back after take-off as in most backward somersaults, but is actually brought forward a little during the take-off and held in this position until the somersault is almost one-half rotated. The legs are starting to flex toward a tuck position immediately after the take-

BACK SOMERSAULT,
FREE POSITION

off. The arms remain uplifted and do not return to meet the knees. The knees are brought up and through the arms. At this time the head is brought back to see the bed and the come-out is made with very little adjustment.

Prerequisite: Backward somersaults in tuck and layout positions.

Forward Somersault with a Half Twist, Tucked or Piked—The half twist is made, as in the barani, when the somersault is one-half completed. The head is ducked forward, however, chin on chest, and the performer can not see the bed at this point. The body is extended as the twist is made, the bed is sighted, and the landing is made on the feet. Forward rotation must be started as forcefully as though no twist is to be made. The safety belt should be employed in learning this skill.

Forward One-and-a-Quarter Somersault with Half Twist to Back-Drop—This exercise may be done in two ways. One is a forward somersault with a half twist overturned to a back-drop landing. The other is a one-and-a-quarter somersault with twist delayed until the last one-quarter somersault. The come-out and twist are then made simultaneously before the landing.

Backward Somersault with Half Twist to Feet—This stunt is most easily executed in the "trampoline back", loose layout position, with a strong take-off. When one-half somersault has been almost completed, the eyes pick up the bed, and at this point the arms are employed to initiate and check the half-twist, and the feet are brought down as in the forward somersault. Care should be taken not to start the twist too early, thus retarding rotation. The safety belt is recommended in learning this twisting technique.

Backward One-and-a-Quarter Somersault with Half Twist to Front-Drop—The somersaulting is done in layout position until the twist is started. The hips and knees are then flexed to keep the feet clear of the bed and to facilitate adjustment of position for the front-drop landing.

BASIC EXERCISES
FROM HANDS AND KNEES TAKE-OFF

Travel Bouncing—Performed the same way as the hands and knees bounce, except that during take-off, the weight is shifted slightly forward, backward, to the right, or to the left, causing the body to travel in any desired direction.

Stretch Bouncing—Immediately after take-off, the body is fully extended in a horizontal position, then the hips and knees are flexed and the arms brought down into position for a hands and knees landing.

Half Twist to Feet—From the take-off, the body is extended to an erect position, and a half-twist to right or left is executed. Landing is made on the feet.

Forward Turnover to Feet—Take-off is made with a vigorous upward thrust of the legs and hips, followed by a tuck. Tuck is released after one-half turn has been completed, and the come-out is made to a feet landing.

Forward Somersault to Hands and Knees—This exercise requires a strong take-off, with emphasis on the upward thrust of the legs and feet. Body must be tightly tucked, and held in that position until the somersault is almost completed. As the tuck is broken, the knees and hips remain partly flexed and the arms are brought forward and down for the landing on hands and knees.

Side-Spins—Side-spins done from a hands and knees take-off involve the same techniques employed in the half and full turntables described under exercises from front-drop take-off.

BASIC EXERCISES FROM KNEES BOUNCE TAKE-OFF

Donkey Kick—A low bounce from the knees is followed by a landing on the hands. As the landing is made, the back is arched and the knees are flexed to absorb shock. This is essentially a low movement, and should never be attempted from a high bounce. (Same as hands bounce.)

Forward Somersault to Feet—This is the least difficult of all full somersaults. At take-off, the arms reach high and are then brought sharply forward and down, drawing the head and shoulders down into a tight tuck position. At the three-quarter point, a quick come-out is made, bringing the body into an erect position for landing on the feet.

Many of the exercises done from a feet take-off—such as forward and backward turnovers and half and full twists to various landing positions—can also be accomplished from the knees take-off position. Since techniques are similar, these exercises will not be discussed in detail. It should be borne in mind, however, that exercises performed from the knees require a strong take-off, and that the legs must be extended immediately after take-off if twists are to be made with the body in a vertical position.

Forward Somersault to Knees—The tuck somersault technique is used to execute three-quarters of the somersault. Then the hips are extended and the knees are kept flexed as the somersault is terminated with a landing on the knees.

Twists—Half and full twists are easily learned from the knees take-off. The knees should be unflexed immediately after take-off so that the body is straight for the twist.

Barani to Knees—This exercise, which should be mastered before the barani from feet take-off to feet is attempted, is best learned by doing round-offs from knees to knees, gradually increasing height and speed of the turnover until it is no longer necessary to use the hands and arms for support. It is important to extend fully as the hips reach a point directly over the center of rotation. The twist should be made *after* extension, not before. As the twist is completed, the legs are brought down, the head and shoulders swing to an erect position, and the knees are flexed for the landing.

BASIC EXERCISES FROM SEAT-DROP TAKE-OFF

Barrel Roll (Full Twist to Seat-Drop)—During the ascent, the body is extended with the shoulders slightly behind and the legs slightly in front of a vertical line passing through the take-off point. The full twist is made as the peak of the bounce is approached. During the drop, the hips are flexed, bringing the torso forward and the legs up into position for landing.

Swivel Hips—See page—72

Backward Somersault to Feet—See page—85

BASIC EXERCISES FROM FRONT-DROP TAKE-OFF

Full Turntable—Action in this exercise is almost identical to that used for Bluch. A more vigorous side-push with the hands is required at take-off, and forceful arm action is required to execute the full side-spin. The legs and hips are more tightly flexed to increase the speed of rotation.

When the full spin is nearly complete, the arms are used to check, and the body is extended for the landing.

Backover to Seat-Drop—Take-off is executed with a strong downward push of the arms and hands. The head and shoulders exert a strong, continuous, backward pull. As soon as the body clears the bed, the knees and hips are flexed, and the knees are drawn up and forward. The hips remain flexed, legs are kicked out, and the hands are brought down and back for a seat-drop landing. This exercise may also be done with back-drop landing.

Backover with Half Twist to Front-Drop—The take-off is identical to that employed in the backover to seat-drop. As the knees are brought forward and the trunk assumes a horizontal position, the body is extended and the arms are used to initiate a half twist in the desired direction. The legs are then brought back and up, the head and shoulders are brought forward and down, and the landing is made in front-drop position.

Back Cody, Tucked (*Front-drop take-off, backward somersault to feet*)—Usually it is easier to learn the cody from the rebound from a "half-back" (threequarter backward somersault) than from any other front-drop landing. It is strongly recommended that, regardless of the preparatory take-off, it be learned in a tumbling belt, or with the assistance of an experienced spotter, as there is otherwise danger of a neck injury resulting from a "hung up" (half completed) cody.

The take-off beat for the cody is of a special type in that the performer is required to land with most of his weight on the thighs and with the knees bent. They continue to bend through the take-off, and even before the bed is fully depressed the hands and arms begin a strong push away from the bed. This thrusting action of the arms is continued until they are fully extended downward. The head is held up and back. As the body leaves the bed the knees straighten for an instant, and then the hips flex, bringing the knees forward to the hands which increases the speed of the backward turnover by thus shortening the radius of rotation. The tucked position is held until the bed comes into view and the come-out is then made to the feet. One and one-quarter somersault is completed in this stunt.

A cody with the come-out to a front-drop can easily be learned after the student becomes consistent in timing the take-off properly as described. With practice he can do it with less and less tuck and can finally do them in lay-out position.

Prerequisites: Practice front-drop to back-drop, making sure to use the front-drop landing described above, in both tuck and lay-out positions, to develop a strong, well-coordinated back-over. Also a high, well-controlled half-back is essential.

Front Cody, Tucked (Forward Turnover to Feet)—The front-drop landing is made with the knees flexed almost at right angles and firmly locked. On contact with the bed the hips begin to flex, driving the bed downward with the knees. The reaction of the bed initiates a forward "tipping" of the body as the take-off is started. As the hip flexion continues the head is ducked under and the hands are brought under and backward to grasp the legs in a tight tuck. This fast, radius-shortening movement increases the speed of rotation. The come-out is made to the feet as approximately three-fourths of a somersault is completed.
Prerequisites: Front-drop, forward turnover to back-drop; mastery of the particular front-drop landing described

above, followed by forward turnover, in tucked position, to a seat-drop.

BASIC EXERCISES FROM BACK-DROP TAKE-OFF

Forward Turnover to Front-Drop—At take-off, the legs are thrust sharply forward, the knees are flexed as the legs are brought under and then thrust backward. The trunk rotates forward and downward, and the body is extended in horizontal position for a front-drop landing.

Half Twist to Front-Drop—At the peak of the bounce, the body is extended, and a half twist to right or left is executed. Feet should be kept a little above the horizontal during the twist. Landing is made in the front-drop position.

Half Twist to Feet—Action in this exercise is identical with that described above up to the point where the half twist has been completed. The hips are then flexed, the legs are brought down, and the landing is made in a bent position. After contact is made, the head and shoulders are raised, placing the body in an erect position.

Cat Twist—This exercise consists of a back-drop take-off, a full twist, and a back-drop landing. The same technique employed in executing a half twist is used here, but is made more forceful to achieve an additional half twist. Feet must be kept high.

Backward Somersault to Back-Drop—This exercise, also known as the backward bounce roll, is accomplished by using a strong backover technique, making a complete turn to a back-drop landing.

Cradle—This exercise consists of a forward turnover with a half twist, followed by a landing in back-drop position. The legs are thrust forward during the take-off, then the knees are flexed and the legs are brought down and under. The twist accompanies this action, and at its completion, the legs and arms are brought up and body position is adjusted for a back-drop landing.

Double Cat Twist—Simultaneously with the high kick-out from the back-drop the hips must start twisting in the desired direction, bringing the front of the body around to face the bed. As the body continues into full extension the arms, which are wide apart, swing into the wrap-up. The head and shoulders overtake, and then lead, the hips in the twisting action through the remainder of the stunt. With practice one learns to anticipate the completion of the double twist, and to adjust for the landing.

Full Twist to Feet—Take-off is accompanied by a forward thrust of the head and legs. As the head and shoulders rise, the body is extended, a full twist is made, and the landing is made on the feet. Twist must be executed while the body is extended.

Porpoise—The porpoise consists of a forward somersault from back-drop take-off to back-drop landing. Take-off is made as for turnover, with head well forward, hips and knees flexed. Turnover continues until body is in position for bent dive to back-drop, then head is ducked for landing. Best control is gained by delaying duck-under until the very last moment.

Ball Out—This is a one-and-a-quarter somersault from back-drop to feet. It requires a strong take-off into a tuck spin. The head must be kept well forward during the spin. Take-off must not be "rushed," and spin must not be started too soon. This causes lack of height.

Kaboom (*Layout back-drop, backover to feet*) —The back-drop is made with the body extended so that the feet are about a foot above the bed as contact is made with the back. The feet are kicked sharply down onto the bed. The reaction of the bed thrusts the legs upward on the rebound. Since the rebound of the upper body has been partially absorbed by the opening action of the kick down, the lower body raises faster than the upper and backward rotation results. A quick tucking of the legs, as in the backover somersault from back-drop position, speeds the rotation to complete a three-quarter somersault to the feet. The use of a safety belt is recommended in learning this stunt.

BASIC EXERCISES FROM HANDS BOUNCE TAKE-OFF

Donkey Kick—The donkey kick from the knees is fully described on the illustrated page headed "Hands Bounce," and is also mentioned under exercises from knees bounce take-off. When done from the feet, the body should be bent forward at the waist to lessen the height of the drop. To do donkey kicks in swing, it is necessary to lengthen the distance between take-off and landing spots, diving slightly forward to the hands. The body does not assume a true vertical handstand position—the center of weight is always kept midway between the take-off and landing spots.

Forward Handspring—In contrast to ground tumbling technique, the arms are not used to gain height by flexion and extension. The recoil of the bed furnishes the necessary lift. The arms are held in full extension as the tumbler employs regular handspring technique. This exercise may be done from either a two-footed or a one-footed take-off.

Back-Drop, Backover to Hands—Following a back-drop, the legs are thrust upward and backward over the head, and the body is extended and arched. The knees are then flexed and the head is thrown back so as to face the bed. The hands are placed on the bed, a hands bounce is executed, and recovery is made to the feet.

Porpoise to Handstand—This is a favorite with hand-balancers. The bounce, from take-off through the forward turnover to the hands, must be kept low and well spotted.

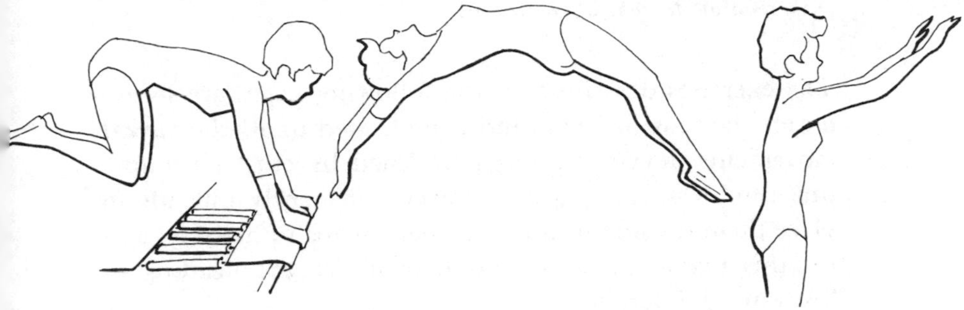

Back Handspring—The same technique is employed here as in ground tumbling. The performer usually has difficulty in keeping low enough to place the proper amount of weight on his hands. This is a great advantage in teaching, however, as it emphasizes the necessity of the backward lean and exaggerates the upward thrust of the hips. After mastering the whip-back somersault, the performer ordinarily has very little trouble learning the back handspring.

7

Advanced Exercises

The next few pages are devoted to descriptions of advanced exercises—exercises more complicated than those previously encountered, and which require a higher degree of proficiency for execution. As in the preceding section, exercises are grouped with relation to take-off positions.

The exercises described on the following pages are by no means the most difficult and complicated of all the varied movements developed and performed by expert trampoline tumblers. They are, however, sufficiently difficult to place them outside of the beginner's scope of activity, and for this reason are discussed here under the heading of "Advanced Exercises."

The problems which the trampoline tumbler faces in executing these more advanced exercises are neither new nor strange. The basic requirements of balance, motion control, and coordination still exist. But, as exercises increase in complexity, the more difficult it becomes to meet these requirements. Action becomes faster and more concentrated. A large number of more advanced skills must be coordinated with greater precision. And here, as always, thorough training in fundamentals, confidence born of experience, and proper aid and supervision—coupled with courage and determination—are the factors which enable the student to meet and master each succeeding exercise.

Tumbling belts, particularly the suspended belt, or "mechanic", illustrated in Chapter Two, are invaluable aids in learning advanced exercises. Using twisting belts now available, it is possible to guide the learner through the most complicated movements with safety. Single, double, or triple somersaults combined with half, full, or multiple twists may be learned in the twisting belt.

In utilizing any form of tumbling belt, it should be kept in mind that the purpose of the belt is not to aid the performer in gaining height or achieving correct timing, but only to guard him from possible injury. Ropes should not be held taut—they should be drawn up only enough to reduce excess slack and keep them from interfering with the tumbler's movements. If the tumbler fails to complete the movement, or appears to be headed for a dangerous landing, the man holding the rope controls the landing by applying his weight to the rope, checking the performer's fall. It goes without saying that rope-holders must be alert, ready, and fully aware of the movements involved before a given exercise is begun.

ADVANCED EXERCISES FROM FEET TAKE-OFF

Forward One-and-Three-Quarter Somersault—Forward rotation is maintained until a one and one-eighth somersault is completed. At this point, a kick-out is made from tuck to pike position, and the head is lifted just enough to slow rotation and enable the tumbler to glimpse the bed. The head is then immediately ducked under for a back-drop landing.

Forward Double Somersault to Seat-Drop—By far the simplest of the double somersaults, this exercise requires good tuck technique combined with a relatively high bounce. After a strong take-off, the tuck is held until the second somersault is almost completed, then a kick-out is made to pike position, and a seat-drop landing is made. Timing is all important in this exercise, which should be thoroughly mastered before the double somersault to feet is attempted.

Forward Double Somersault to Feet—A strong, well-balanced take-off is essential for a double somersault. It is best to practice with a mechanic tumbling belt if available —otherwise a double-rope belt will suffice. The somersault spin is continued to the same point described for the double to seat-drop. A come-out is made instead of a kick-out, and the feet are brought downward and under the center of weight. The tuck should never be held until the landing is made. It is better to come out too early than too late.

Backward Double Somersault to Feet—To accomplish a backward double somersault, the performer must be able to control single somersaults with exceptional height and a fast spin. He must also be able to do a high layout somersault. The backward double somersault is started with the same lift and backward throw of the head and arms as employed in the backward layout somersault. This starts the body rotating backward while fully extended. A tight tuck is then employed to increase the speed of rotation, and the head continues to drive backward until the second somersault is almost completed. The come-out is made as in the single backward somersault. If the take-off and tuck actions are good, the second somersault will be faster than the first. As in the forward double somersault, the timing of the come-out is largely a matter of muscle memory. The performer can, however, see the bed before making his landing. The tumbling belt should be employed until the exercise has been completely mastered.

Forward Somersault with Full Twist to Feet—Forward rotation is started in semi-tuck or open pike position. When the head is directly under the center of rotation, the body is straightened and the full twist is made. The head and shoulders continue up and forward, and the feet are brought down for the landing.

Backward Somersault with Full Twist—The take-off is very similar to that for the layout back somersault. It is made with a straight forward and upward swing of the extended arms a little more than shoulder width apart. The hips are thrust forward and the head and shoulders are brought backward extending the body into a position slightly less arched than in the layout somersault. This is because the head is not forced back as far. It is thrust back very little from its normal "face forward" position in relation to the chest and shoulders. The "lay back" action here is done practically "all in one piece" as far as the shoulders and head are concerned. At the point of complete extension, with the face and chest upward, the right arm is thrown forcefully over to the left, across in front of the chest. The head and shoulders turn in the direction of the twist, keeping themselves aligned with the longitudinal axis. The hips and lower body follow with legs extended, firmly together, and toes pointed.

Simultaneously with the action of the right arm the left arm bends sharply as the elbow is brought downward and backward and, as the body rolls into it, the arm is brought in close to the front of the chest near the right arm. This not only speeds the twisting action but also adds force to the backward rotation.

The first quarter turn of the head and shoulders allows the performer to see the bed. As the twist continues, the somersault also continues, and the performer is able to see the bed throughout the remainder of the stunt. The twist is completed when the somersault is approximately three-fourths finished. At this point the hips are flexed and the arms are spread to stop the twist and bring the feet down for the landing.

The mechanic twisting belt should be used in learning this "back full," as it is so aptly called.

If a twisting belt is not available a different learning procedure can be employed. This involves over-twisting the half-twisting back somersault to a three-quarter twist and progressively adding a little more twist until a complete twist is accomplished. This takes more trial and error experimenting, and the resulting twist is not likely to be as smooth and efficient as the first.

Prerequisites: A well-controlled layout back somersault; good half-twisting back somersault technique; full twist to back-drop; barrel roll; double twist to back-drop.

Backward One-and-a-Quarter Somersault with Full Twist to Back-Drop—This skill consists of the basic exercise, "backward one-and-a-quarter somersault with half twist," with an additional half twist. The last half twist is added during the drop in front- drop position, converting it to a back-drop. It may also be done by over-turning a backward somersault with full twist to back-drop.

Backward One-and-Three-Quarter Somersault with Half Twist to Back-Drop—The half-twisting backward somersault must be rotated very fast to allow time for the head to be ducked forward and under for the additional turnover to a back-drop landing. The hips and legs are flexed immediately after the twist to speed up forward rotation.

Rudolph (Forward Somersault with One-and-One-Half Twist. Twisting to Left) —The take-off for the Rudolph

RUDOLPH
(Forward Somersault with One-and-One-Half Twists)

is almost the same as for the barani. There is a little less forward bending into the pike position and the arms are held wider apart. The emphasis is upon a strong lifting of the hips and legs, without ducking the head, to start the forward rotation. Immediately upon becoming airborne—before maximum height is reached—the right arm is swung forcefully downward past the front of the knees and continued across the chest toward the left shoulder. Simultaneously with this arm action the piked position is opened, straightening the body to facilitate, by the transfer of momentum, fast twisting action on the longitudinal axis. The left arm, elbow leading the twist, bends as the body rolls into it for the wrap-up with both fore-arms close to each other at the chest. Care should be taken to avoid leading with the head looking over the shoulder. For just an instant the performer loses sight of the bed during the first part of the twisting movement. Then he sees it again and continues to see it throughout the remainder of the stunt. If all movements are correctly timed he soon comes to feel that he sees it all the time. This allows the performer to hold the wrap-up with confidence until he has almost completed the one and one half twist and is turning to face the bed with the front of his body.

He makes a controlled come-out, checking the twist by bending at the hips and opening his arms to the sides as he brings his feet down for the landing.

Prerequisites: The barani, the half-twisting forward somersault, and the full-twisting forward somersault are considered minimum requirements. Twisting stunts such as the barrel roll, cat twist, corkscrew and the double twist to a back-drop are recommended for mastering the twisting used in the successful performance of the Rudolph and other advanced twisting moves. Use of the twisting safety belt is advisable.

Backward Somersault with Double Twist (Back Double Full—Twisting to the Left)—The full twisting backward somersault is the logical base from which to progress toward the double twisting back somersault. After becoming consistently skillful in executing fast-spinning, high-finishing back fulls with ease, control, and good form, the trampolinist can consider himself ready to add another twist. This is accomplished in the belt. The best, easiest, fastest, and only safe way to learn this, or any other multiple twisting stunt, is in the suspended twisting belt in the arms of our old friend—the mechanic.

During the take-off the arms are wide apart in their upward swing and there is a slight anticipatory twisting to the left initiated in the upper body just before the feet leave the bed. All of the actions described for the "back full" are brought into play with more emphasis on twisting and less on backward rotation.

The backward thrusting force derived through the transfer of momentum from the twisting action of the arms is the compensatory factor. The arms, after initiating the twist, arrive in a position in front of the chest. They are held there longer and closer to the body than in the Back Full, shortening the radius of momentum to increase the speed of the twist.

To obtain an efficient, smooth twisting spin the body is kept fully extended with no arch or flexion and with the legs firmly together and toes pointed.

The eyes see the bed early, just as in the Back Full, and they continue to see it throughout all, or most of, the stunt. As the second twist is completed, the hips are flexed for the landing and the arms and legs spread sideward to further check the twist.

Prerequisites: Back Full, and back somersault with one and one half twist.

Barani Out Fliffis (Forward Double Somersault with Half Twist in Second Somersault. Twist Described is to the Left)—The take-off into the forward rotation is the same as for a double forward somersault with slightly more

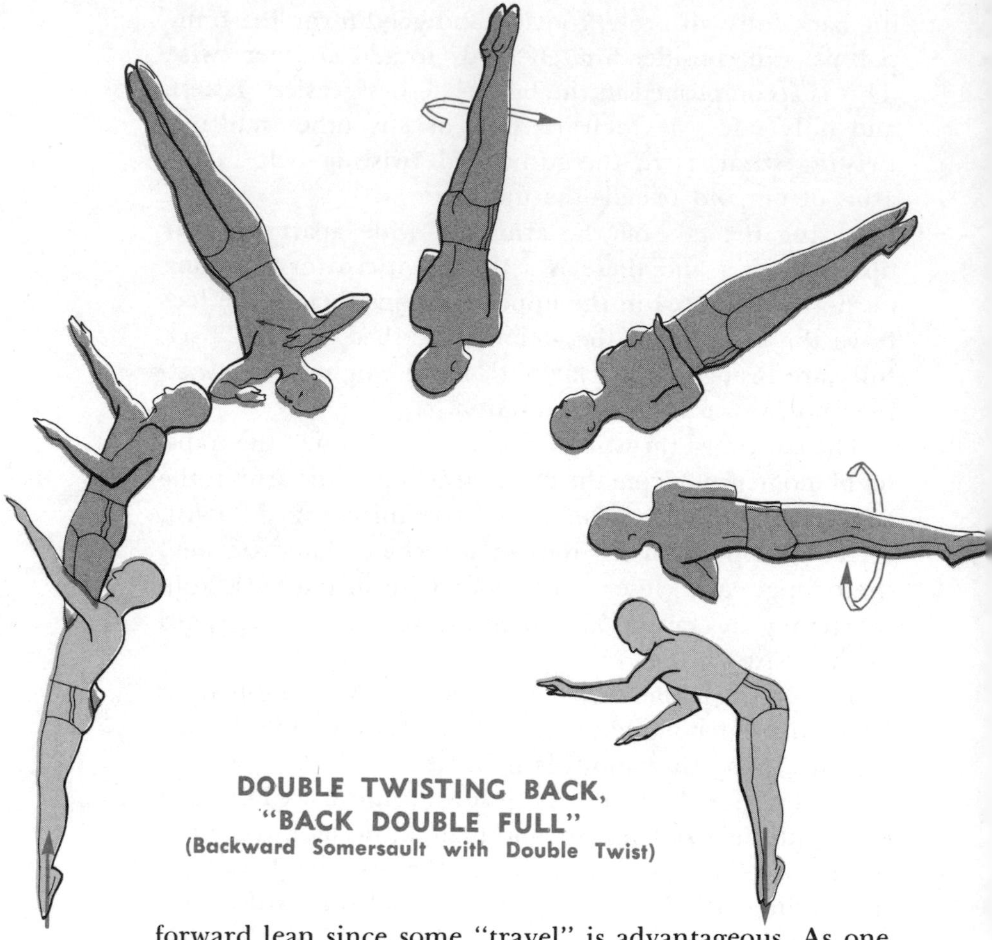

DOUBLE TWISTING BACK, "BACK DOUBLE FULL"
(Backward Somersault with Double Twist)

forward lean since some "travel" is advantageous. As one and one-half somersault is completed a kick-out is made from tuck to pike position, the bed is sighted, and the barani is made to finish the stunt. The speed of rotation is slowed down by the kick-out and it is necessary for the individual trampolinist to decide through practice—trial and error method—just when to kick-out and how much he needs to raise his head to see the bed, which also slows rotation. This can best be learned by simply releasing the

BARANI OUT FLIFFIS
(Forward Double Somersault with One-Half Twist In Second Somersault)

tuck and continuing through the barani in a semi-tucked or free position until confident and ready for the kick-out style.

Prerequisites: Barani; half-twisting front somersault; barani from back-drop to feet; one and three quarter front; double front somersault.

Barani In Fliffis, "Half In Fliffis" (Forward Double Somersault with a Half Twist in the First Somersault)—This stunt requires a strong high bounce take-off with fast forward rotation in the barani movement. The last half of the barani is done with the hips and knees flexing into the tuck position. The tuck is completed just before the first somer-

BARANI IN FLIFFIS
(Forward Double Somersault with One-Half Twist In First Somersault)

sault is finished. The head is back to see the bed and, as it comes into view, the come-out is made for the landing.

Prerequisites: Barani overturned to back-drop, using a very low bounce in order to force a fast tuck; an early twisting ball-out barani; overturned early twisting cradle; practice of completed stunt from diving-board.

Back Full Fliffis (Half in, Half Out. Backward Double

BACK FULL FLIFFIS,
"HALF IN, HALF OUT"

Somersault with a Half Twist in the First Somersault and a Half Twist in the Second Somersault) —The first half-twist is started immediately on the take-off and is completed while the body is still rising and flexing toward a tuck. As the half twist is completed the body is a little more than half way through the first somersault and the head is brought forward for the temporary tuck, held just until the bed is sighted. Then the hips and knees are extended for the "barani out" action to the feet. After the take-off all of the movements must be hurried in order to complete the first revolution and the first half twist before the body starts its descent. Therefore, the foot thrust must be forceful enough to accommodate a strong rotation of the straight body and also to initiate the twist.

Prerequisites: Controlled, low back somersault with early half twist and quick tuck to feet called "Arabian Half Twister" in ground tumbling; back one-and-a-quarter somersault with early half twist to front-drop; back one-and-three-quarter with half twist; the learner should practice the entire stunt in the mechanic twisting belt until confident.

ADVANCED EXERCISES FROM FRONT-DROP TAKE-OFF

Double Back Cody, Tucked—After thoroughly mastering the single back cody and the layout back cody to the feet, the next step is to practice increasing the speed of rotation of both skills. When the tucked cody can be overturned to the back-drop position the performer is ready to attempt the double cody in the belt. It is then only a matter of sufficient height and correct timing to accomplish the entire stunt. Care should be taken to avoid touching the bed with the feet as the legs are whipped forward, for the tuck, from the take-off position.

Full Twisting Back Cody ("Back Full Cody")—During the take-off the twisting is initiated by the thrusting action of the arms and hands against the bed. The recoil force of the bed is transferred through the arms to the head and shoulders in the direction of the twist as well as upward and backward. As the body rises to the vertical

FULL TWISTING BACK CODY
(Front Drop)

position the arms are brought across the lower chest for the wrap-up for the full twist and the one-and-one-quarter somersault is continued to completion to the feet. The mechanic twisting belt should be used to learn this stunt.

Prerequisites: Well-controlled layout back cody to feet; also to front-drop; good techniques in back somersaults with half, full one-and-a-half, and double twists; half twisting back cody, in belt.

ADVANCED EXERCISES FROM BACK-DROP TAKE-OFF

Corkscrew—This exercise involves a forward turnover from a back-drop take-off, a one-and-a-half twist, and a back-drop landing. The body must be extended completely as a strong turnover is executed. A full twist is executed as the body passes through a vertical position and an additional half twist is added as the turnover continues, placing the body in position for a back-drop landing. This exercise is difficult to accomplish because it requires both height and forward rotation in layout position.

Ball Out Barani—The rebound from the back-drop should be moderately high so that the forward rotation to the head-down position of the body can be reached before the peak is reached. This rotation is started as in the "ball out" to feet, with head ducked forward. When the body is almost into the head-down position the performer looks for the bed and does the barani twist come-out to his feet. A few times in the safety belt is usually sufficient to learn when to break out for the twist. It is called the "baby fliffis", and is the most important step toward the Barani Out.

Ball Out with Full Twist—This is a "porpoise" with a full twist, also known as a "full twisting ball out." It is recommended that the full twist from back-drop to front-drop, well controlled from a high forward dive, be considered a prerequisite. Then, with the aid of the twist ing belt it can be safely learned by overturning forward rotation and ducking the head to land on the back.

Double Ball Out—This is accomplished by overturning

the "ball out to feet," requiring a tight tuck, and making the come-out exactly as in the one-and-three-quarter forward somersault.

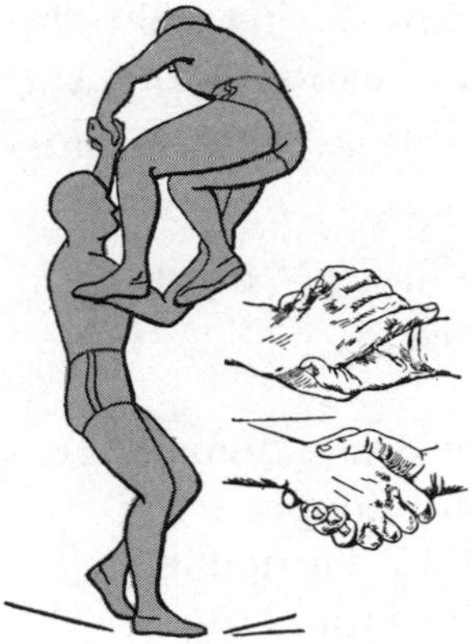

8

Glossary of Exercises

A list of 51 exercises is presented here, grouped on the basis of their levels of difficulty to provide an index for competitive and class scoring. Also the Table of Difficulty Rating, used in international competitions, is provided as a comprehensive listing of stunts at all levels.

1. Straight Bounce ½ Twist.
2. Tuck Bounce.
3. Pike Bounce.
4. Arch-Out or Swan Bounce.
5. Pike Straddle Bounce.
6. Front-Drop, ½ Turntable.
7. Swan Dive to Front-Drop.
8. Seat-Drop, ½ Twist to Feet.
9. Seat-Drop, Frontover to Front-Drop.
10. Swivel Hips.
11. Pirouette (full twist).
12. One Half Twist to Front-Drop.
13. One Half Twist to Back-Drop.
14. Hands and Knees, Frontover to Back-Drop.
15. Turntable.
16. Front-Drop, Backover to Back-Drop (or reverse).
17. Swan Dive to Front-Drop.

18. Jack-Knife Dive to Front-Drop.
19. Donkey Kick (hands bounce, snap to feet).
20. Back-Drop ½ Twist to Feet.
21. Pirouette-and-a-Half (Straight bounce with 1½ twist).
22. Bent Dive (frontover to back-drop).
23. Swan Dive to Back-Drop.
24. Jack-Knife to Back-Drop.
25. Back-Drop, Full Twist to Feet.
26. Cat Twist (Back-Drop, Full Twist, Back-Drop).
27. Back-Drop, Backover to Feet (Tuck, pike, or layout).
28. Half Back (¾ backward somersault to front-drop).
29. Back-Drop, Backover to Hands (Hold handstand or snap down to feet).
30. Back-Drop, Frontover to Hands (only for strong hand-balancers).
31. Cradle (Back-drop, frontover ½ twist to back-drop).
32. Knees Bounce, Forward Somersault, Tucked, to Feet.
33. Forward Somersault, Tuck.
34. Backward Somersault, Tuck or Free.
35. Porpoise (Ballout with arch-out frontover to back-drop).
36. One-and-a-Half Twist to Back-Drop.
37. Hands and Knees, Forward Somersault to Hands and Knees or to Front-Drop.
38. Double Turntable.
39. Three-Quarter Backward Somersault with One-Half Twist.
40. Back Cody to Front-Drop, Tuck or Free.
41. Front Cody to Front-Drop, Tuck or Free.
42. Barani.
43. Corkscrew.

44. Forward Somersault with One-Half Twist, Free.
45. Back Cody to Feet.
46. Backward One and One-Quarter Somersault, Tuck.
47. Forward One-and-One-Quarter Somersault.
48. Ballout to Feet, Tuck.
49. Backward Somersault with One-Half Twist, Free.
50. Three-Quarter Backward Somersault with a Full Twist.
51. Forward or Backward Somersault, Pike, Flying or Layout.

DIFFICULTY RATINGS

Starting Positions

		Feet					Seat					Stomach					Back				
Somersault	Twist	Forward	Backward		Pike	Layout	Forward	Backward		Pike	Layout	Forward	Backward		Pike	Layout	Forward	Backward		Pike	Layout
Tuck jump				1																	
Pike jump				1																	
Pike straddle jump				1																	
Split jump				1																	
All similar jumps without twists				1																	
Seat bounce				1					1												
Turntables																					
½														1							
1														2							
1-½														3							
2														4							
0	½	—	—	1	—	—	—	—		—	—	—	—	1	—	—	—	—	1	—	—
0	1	—	—	2	—	—	—	—	2	—	—	—	—	2	—	—	—	—	2	—	—
0	1-½	—	—	3	—	—	—	—		—	—	—	—	3	—	—	—	—	3	—	—
0	2	—	—	4	—	—	—	—	4	—	—	—	—	4	—	—	—	—	4	—	—
0	2-½	—	—	5	—	—	—	—		—	—	—	—	5	—	—	—	—	5	—	—
0	3	—	—	6	—	—	—	—	6	—	—	—	—	6	—	—	—	—	6	—	—
¼	0	1	1		—	—	—	—		—	—	—	1		—	—	1	—		—	—
¼	½	2	2		—	—	2	—		—	—	—	2		—	—	2	—		—	—
¼	1	3	3		—	—	—	—		—	—	—	3		—	—	3	—		—	—
¼	1-½	4	4		—	—	4	—		—	—	—	4		—	—	4	—		—	—
¼	2	5	5		—	—	—	—		—	—	—	5		—	—	5	—		—	—
¼	2-½	6	6		—	—	6	—		—	—	—	6		—	—	6	—		—	—
¼	3	7	7		—	—	—	—		—	—	—	7		—	—	7	—		—	—

½	0	—	—	—	—	—	—	—	—	2	2	—	—	2	2	—	—
½	½	—	—	—	—	—	—	—	—	3	3	—	—	3	3	—	—
½	1	—	—	—	—	—	—	—	—	4	4	—	—	4	4	—	—
½	1-½	—	—	—	—	—	—	—	—	5	5	—	—	5	5	—	—
½	2	—	—	—	—	—	—	—	—	6	6	—	—	6	6	—	—
½	2-½	—	—	—	—	—	—	—	—	7	7	—	—	7	7	—	—
½	3	—	—	—	—	—	—	—	—	8	8	—	—	8	8	—	—
¾	0	3	3	4*	4*	3	3	—	—	3	—	—	—	—	3	—	—
¾	½	4	4	Free		4	4	—	—	4	—	—	—	—	4	—	—
¾	1	5	5	Free		5	5	—	—	5	—	—	—	—	5	—	—
¾	1-½	6	6	Free		6	6	—	—	6	—	—	—	—	6	—	—
¾	2	7	7	Free		7	7	—	—	7	—	—	—	—	7	—	—
¾	2-½	8	8	Free		8	8	—	—	8	—	—	—	—	8	—	—
¾	3	9	9	Free		9	9	—	—	9	—	—	—	—	9	—	—
* Backward only																	
1	0	4	4	5	5	4	4	—	—	4	4	5	5	4	4	—	—
1	½	5	5	Free		5	5	—	—	5	5	—	—	5	5	—	—
1	1	6	6	Free		6	6	—	—	6	6	—	—	6	6	—	—
1	1-½	7	7	Free		7	7	—	—	7	7	—	—	7	7	—	—
1	2	8	8	Free		8	8	—	—	8	8	—	—	8	8	—	—
1	2-½	9	9	Free		9	9	—	—	9	9	—	—	9	9	—	—
1	3	10	10	Free		10	10	—	—	10	10	—	—	—	—	—	—
1	3-½	11	11	Free		—	—	—	—	—	—	—	—	—	—	—	—
1	4	12	12	Free		—	—	—	—	—	—	—	—	—	—	—	—
1-¼	0	5	5	6	6	—	—	—	—	—	5	6	6	5	—	—	—
1-¼	½	6	6	Free		6	—	—	—	—	6	—	—	6	—	—	—
1-¼	1	7	7	Free		—	—	—	—	—	7	—	—	7	—	—	—
1-¼	1-½	8	8	Free		8	—	—	—	—	8	—	—	8	—	—	—
1-¼	2	9	9	Free		—	—	—	—	—	9	—	—	9	—	—	—
1-¼	2-½	10	10	Free		10	—	—	—	—	10	—	—	10	—	—	—
1-¼	3	11	11	Free		—	—	—	—	—	11	—	—	11	—	—	—
1-¼	3-½	12	12	Free		—	—	—	—	—	12	—	—	12	—	—	—
1-¼	4	13	13	Free		—	—	—	—	—	13	—	—	—	—	—	—
1-½	0	—	—	—	—	—	—	—	—	6	6	7	7	6	6	—	—
1-½	½	—	—	—	—	—	—	—	—	7	7	—	—	7	7	—	—
1-½	1	—	—	—	—	—	—	—	—	8	8	—	—	8	8	—	—
1-½	1-½	—	—	—	—	—	—	—	—	9	9	—	—	9	9	—	—
1-½	2	—	—	—	—	—	—	—	—	10	10	—	—	10	10	—	—
1-½	2-½	—	—	—	—	—	—	—	—	11	11	—	—	11	11	—	—
1-½	3	—	—	—	—	—	—	—	—	12	12	—	—	12	12	—	—
1-½	3-½	—	—	—	—	—	—	—	—	13	13	—	—	—	—	—	—
1-½	4	—	—	—	—	—	—	—	—	—	—	—	—	—	—	—	—

		Feet				Seat				Stomach				Back			
Somersault	Twist	Forward	Backward	Pike	Layout	Forward	Backward	Pike	Layout	Forward	Backward	Pike	Layout	Forward	Backward	Pike	Layout
				For, Back PL	PL												
1-¾	0	7	9	8 8	10 10	7	7	—	—	7	—	8	8	—	7	—	—
1-¾	½	8	8	Free	Free	8	8	—	—	8	—	—	—	—	8	—	—
1-¾	1	9	11	Free	Free	9	9	—	—	9	—	—	—	—	9	—	—
1-¾	1-½	10	10	Free	Free	10	10	—	—	10	—	—	—	—	10	—	—
1-¾	2	11	13	Free	Free	—	—	—	—	—	—	—	—	—	11	—	—
1-¾	2-½	12	12	Free	Free	—	—	—	—	—	—	—	—	—	—	—	—
1-¾	3	13	15	Free	Free	—	—	—	—	—	—	—	—	—	—	—	—
1-¾	3-½	14	14	Free	Free	—	—	—	—	—	—	—	—	—	—	—	—
2	0	8	8	9	9	8	8	—	—	8	8	9	9	8	8	—	—
2	½	9	9	Free		9	9	—	—	9	9	—	—	9	9	—	—
2	1	10	10	Free		—	—	—	—	10	10	—	—	10	10	—	—
2	1-½	11	11	Free		—	—	—	—	—	11	—	—	11	—	—	—
2	2	12	12	Free		—	—	—	—	—	12	—	—	12	—	—	—
2	2-½	13	13	Free		—	—	—	—	—	—	—	—	—	—	—	—
2	3	14	14	Free		—	—	—	—	—	—	—	—	—	—	—	—
2	3-½	15	15	Free		—	—	—	—	—	—	—	—	—	—	—	—
2-¼	0	9	9	10	10	—	—	—	—	—	9	10	10	9	—	—	—
2-¼	½	10	10	Free		—	—	—	—	—	10	—	—	10	—	—	—
2-¼	1	11	11	Free		—	—	—	—	—	11	—	—	11	—	—	—
2-¼	1-½	—	—	—	—	—	—	—	—	—	12	—	—	12	—	—	—
2-¼	2	—	—	—	—	—	—	—	—	—	13	—	—	—	—	—	—
2-½	0	—	—	—	—	—	—	—	—	10	10	11	11	10	10	—	—
2-½	½	—	—	—	—	—	—	—	—	11	11	—	—	11	11	—	—
2-½	1	—	—	—	—	—	—	—	—	12	12	—	—	12	12	—	—
				For Back PL	PL												
2-¾	0	11	13	12	14	—	—	—	—	—	—	—	—	—	—	—	—
2-¾	½	12	12	Free	Free	—	—	—	—	—	—	—	—	—	—	—	—
2-¾	1	13	15	Free	Free	—	—	—	—	—	—	—	—	—	—	—	—
3	0	12	12	13	13	—	—	—	—	—	12	—	—	12	—	—	—
3	½	13	—	Free		—	—	—	—	—	—	—	—	—	—	—	—
3	1	14	14	Free		—	—	—	—	—	—	—	—	—	—	—	—
3	1-½	15	—	Free		—	—	—	—	—	—	—	—	—	—	—	—
3-¼	0	13	13	14	14	—	—	—	—	—	13	—	—	13	—	—	—

9

Suggested Routines

The routines listed below—selected from the wide variety of combined exercises which may be performed on the trampoline—are arranged progressively with regard to difficulty of execution. They are presented here to illustrate the wide range of accomplishment open to the versatile trampoline tumbler, and to suggest and stimulate the origination of additional routines.

The faultless execution of combined exercises constitutes the peak of achievement in trampoline tumbling. In executing routines, the trampoline tumbler is faced with new problems in addition to all those regularly encountered in the performance of individual exercises. Continuous and protracted action complicates the difficulties encountered in the execution of routines. Greater demands are placed upon muscle memory. Each individual exercise which is included in the routine must be executed flawlessly, landings must be made in exactly the right position for beginning the next exercise, spotting must be perfect. The entire sequence of movements involved in the routine must be firmly fixed in the performer's mind for—as previously noted in the introduction to the section dealing with fundamental body mechanics—once the first exercise has been initiated, there is no time to pause, select, or ponder. Execution must be perfectly and automatically coordinated, if continuity is to be maintained.

A routine is not a haphazard combination of exercises. In devising routines, certain factors must be kept in mind with regard to the selection of exercises to be included and the sequence of their performance within the routine. Spotting becomes a primary consideration—exercises must be carefully selected and arranged in a specific order, so that action can be concentrated near the center of the bed. The feasibility of executing various exercises from certain landing and take-off positions and the height of bounce and relative effort required to perform component exercises have definite bearing on the composition of routines.

Combinations of exercises may be devised which are suitable for students at all levels of proficiency. Routines may be as simple or as advanced as the instructor desires, ranging from a simple combination of the seven fundamental bounces—widely employed as a warm-up procedure —to a complicated series of twisting somersaults. Regardless of their simplicity or difficulty, in the origination and execution of routines both instructors and students will find ample opportunity for the application of initiative and ingenuity, and for the development and demonstration of ability.

FUNDAMENTAL PRACTICE ROUTINES

1. Knees, Hands, Feet, Seat-Drop, Feet; Repeat.
2. Knees, Front-Drop, Knees, Hands, Knees, Back-Drop, Feet.
3. Swivel Hips in Swing.
4. Half Turntables in Swing.
5. Front-Drop, Hands and Knees, Hands, Feet, Seat-Drop, Back-Drop, Feet.
6. Back-Drop, Half Twist, Feet: Repeat in Swing.

7. Forward Somersault to Seat-Drop, Feet, Seat-Drop, Feet: Repeat in Swing.
8. Forward Somersault, Free Bounce, Half Twist, Free Bounce: Repeat.
9. Backward Somersault, Free Bounce: Repeat in Swing.
10. Backward Somersault, Free Bounce, Forward Somersault, Free Bounce: Repeat in Swing.
11. Back-Drop, Backover to Feet, Bent Dive to Back-Drop, Feet: Repeat in Swing.
12. Cradles in Swing, Finishing with Porpoise.
13. Half Back, Backover to Back-Drop, Cat Twist, Feet: Repeat in Swing.
14. Bent Dive to Back-Drop, Porpoise, Half Twist to Feet, Free Bounce, Backward Somersault, Forward Somersault, Full Twist.
15. Backward Somersault, Forward Somersault: Repeat in Swing.
16. Backward Somersault in Swing.
17. Backward Somersault, Barany, Free Bounce: Repeat in Swing.
18. Baranies in Swing.
19. Backward Somersault, Barany: Repeat in Swing.
20. One-and-a-Quarter to Front-Drop, Half Turntable, Backover to Back-Drop, Cat Twist, Feet.
21. Backward Somersault with Half Twist, Free Bounce: Repeat in Swing.
22. Backward Somersault, Forward One-and-Three-Quarter Somersault, Ball-Out to Feet, Free Bounce, Backward Somersault.
23. One-and-a-Quarter Backward Somersault to Back-Drop, Backover to Back-Drop, Feet, Back-Drop, Porpoise, Feet, Full Twist.

24. One-and-a-Quarter Backward Somersault with Half Twist to Front-Drop, Free Bounce: Repeat in Swing.
25. Backward Somersault with Full Twist, Free Bounce: Repeat in Swing.
26. Backward Somersault with Full Twist, Backward Somersault: Repeat in Swing.

INTERMEDIATE ROUTINES

(With total value of difficulty given in parenthesis)

1. 2 back, back full, tucked back, barani, double full, piked back, rudolph, layout back, $\frac{3}{4}$ front, cradle back to feet. (5.7)
2. $1\frac{3}{4}$ front, ballout barani, layout back, back full, $\frac{3}{4}$ back, tucked cody, rudolph, piked back, barani, double back. (5.7)
3. $1\frac{3}{4}$ back, tucked cody, piked back, barani, back full, tucked back, rudolph, layout back, $1\frac{3}{4}$ front, rudolph ballout. (5.9)
4. Barani out fliffis, piked back, rudolph, double full, $\frac{3}{4}$ back, cody full, barani, tucked back, back full, 2 back. (6.2)
5. Double full, rudolph, back full, piked back, 2 back, tucked back, $1\frac{3}{4}$ front, barani ball-out, barani, barani out fliffis. (6.5)

ADVANCED ROUTINES

(With total value of difficulty given in parenthesis)

1. 2 back, double full, barani out fliffis, rudolph, tucked back, $1\frac{3}{4}$ forward som., barani ball-out, back full, $\frac{3}{4}$ back, tucked cody. (6.3)

2. Barani out fliffis, 2 back, tucked back, back full, rudolph, layout back, double full, piked back, 1¾ forward som., ballout to feet. (6.4)
3. Barani in fliffis, Barani out fliffis, tucked back, double back, rudolph, double full, back full, piked back, 1¾ forward som., rudolph ball-out. (7.1)
4. Back full fliffis, barani out fliffis, tucked back, back full, barani in fliffis, 2 back, rudolph, piked back, 1¾ back, 2 cody. (7.4)
5. Late rudolph fliffis, tucked back, 1¾ back, Cody with full twist, rudolph, double back, barani out fliffis, back full, double full, triple full. (7.7)
6. Triple full, 2 back, rudolph, double full, barani out fliffis, 1¾ back, 2 cody, back tucked, back full, barani in fliffis. (7.7)
7. Triple full, rudolph, piked back, barani out fliffis, randolph, back full, ½ in—½ out fliffis, tucked back, 2¾ forward som., ball-out with full. (7.8)
8. Full in—barani out fliffis, back full, piked 2 back, double full, piked back, 1¾ back, double full cody, tucked back, 2 back, 3 back. (7.9)
9. 3 back, piked barani out fliffis, 2 back, back full, ½ in—½ out fliffis, rudolph, randolph, piked back, 1¾ back with full twist, 2 cody. (8.5)

Key to Abbreviations:

2 Back—Double back somersault.
3 Back—Triple back somersault.
2 Cody—Double back cody.
Cradle back—Ball-out with very early ½ twist.
Late rudolph fliffis—The entire 1½ twists are in last somersault.

10

Group Tumbling

ALTERNATE BOUNCING

Trampoline tumbling is most generally practiced as a solo sport—one in which a single performer occupies the center of the stage, and in which proficiency is governed by the ability of the individual alone. There are, however, many exercises and routines which may be accomplished by two or more participants, performing at the same time on a single trampoline. Group tumbling of this nature involves certain additional skills (alternate bouncing, simultaneous bouncing, over-and under bouncing, and shoulder mounts and dismounts) and introduces an element not present in solo trampoline tumbling—teamwork. Problems of timing, balance, and spotting are amplified, and cooperation becomes a prime factor along with coordination.

In alternate bouncing, the importance of controlling and spotting each bounce becomes immediately apparent. It is equally essential that both performers keep their bounces equal in height to facilitate timing. Almost all alternate bouncing exercises and routines are prefaced by straight bouncing, which enables the performers to coordinate the height and rhythm of their bounces. Bounces must be alternated—so timed that one performer is at the top of his bounce while the other is at the lowest point. If timing is off, both performers should check and start over.

In performing alternate bouncing exercises or routines, bounces are first coordinated; then one performer—previously designated as lead-off man—"cues in" his partner by calling "Right!", "Set!", or some similar word one full bounce before the actual exercise or routine is to be started. Partners must have all movements of the exercise or routine definitely fixed in their minds before bouncing is started. It will be found that moderately high bounces are easiest to control and coordinate, and care must be taken at all times to avoid interference due to faulty timing.

Suggested exercises and routines involving alternate bouncing are listed and described in detail below and on the next page. Succeeding pages are devoted to explanation of the techniques involved in simultaneous bouncing, over-and-under bouncing, and shoulder mounts and dismounts.

ALTERNATE BOUNCING EXERCISES AND ROUTINES

Straight Bouncing—Participants face each other in starting position for feet bounce. As "A"—the lead-off man—starts his bounce, "B" absorbs bed recoil by flexing his knees, then starts his bounce as "A" reaches his highest point of bounce. Bounces should be spotted midway between the center and the ends of the bed. Tucks, pikes, or half and full twists may be incorporated for variation.

Fundamental Bounces with Free Bounce—After straight bounces have been coordinated, "A" does a knees bounce --or any other fundamental bounce except the feet bounce —followed by a free bounce. "B" starts a free bounce while "A" is at the peak of his knees bounce, and follows with a knees bounce. A feet bounce with any of the variations listed in the paragraph above may be employed in place of the free bounce.

Teeter-Totter—"A" starts with a seat-drop executed with the legs well apart in a straddle position; "B" starts with a seat-drop done in the regular manner. As "A" descends and "B" ascends, "B's" feet pass between "A's" legs. Both "A" and "B" then execute free bounces, then "B" does a straddle seat-drop and "A" a regular seat-drop, "A's" feet passing between "B's" legs during the bounce.

Straddle Seat-Drop and Front-Drop with Free Bounce—"A" does a straddle seat-drop, a front-drop, and a free bounce. "B" does a front-drop, a free bounce, and a straddle seat-drop, synchronized with "A's" routine. Note that in each case the free bounce follows the front-drop.

Straddle Seat-Drop and Front-Drop—Same as above, except that free bounces are omitted.

Backward or Forward Somersault with Free Bounce—"A" executes a somersault—forward or backward—followed by a free bounce. "B" does a free bounce, then duplicates the somersault performed by his partner.

Forward and Backward Somersaults with Free Bounce—"A" does a forward somersault, a free bounce, a backward somersault, and another free bounce. "B" executes the same routine with proper synchronization.

Backward or Forward Somersaults in Swing—Free bounces are omitted in this exercise, each participant alternating in the execution of identical somersaults in swing.

SIMULTANEOUS BOUNCING

Another skill widely employed in group tumbling is simultaneous bouncing. Here two performers execute bounces in unison—not alternately, as was the case in alternate bouncing.

Certain of the comments made in the section on alternate bouncing with regard to the importance of controlling and spotting each bounce, maintaining equal height of bounce, and checking when timing is faulty have equal application to simultaneous bouncing. There are, however, major differences between the two techniques. In simultaneous bouncing, both participants must work the bed at the same time, and in the same manner. Coordination must be even more exact than in alternate bouncing. Because of the difficulty in achieving absolutely perfect coordination, it is recommended that only low bounces be employed, to minimize cast which may result from comparatively minor errors in timing.

Since both performers work the bed at the same time, the bed and springs are subjected to double their normal load. This extra weight may depress the bed too far during some exercises, causing the performers to hit the bottom cross-frame. Bed set, therefore, should always be checked before simultaneous bouncing is attempted. A safe rule, which protects both the equipment and the participants, is to adjust the bed set for a load equal to the combined weights of both performers.

All of the fundamental bounces—together with simple variations, forward turnovers, and backovers—may be employed in simultaneous bouncing. In general, exercises are performed in one of the following positions: (1) Face-to-face, in which the participants face each other and clasp hands; (2) Side-by-side, in which participants stand side by side, both facing in the same direction, with their inside arms locked and hands clasped; or (3) Tandem, in which the participants stand one behind the other, facing in the same direction, with the rear man grasping his partner's forearms. Some of the simpler exercises and routines which may be performed simultaneously by two tumblers are listed on the next page.

SIMULTANEOUS BOUNCING EXERCISES AND ROUTINES

Face-to-Face Knees Bounce—Partners face each other, extend their arms, and clasp hands. Both begin with free bounces, then—when timing has been established—execute the knees bounce in unison. For variation, feet bounces and knees bounces may be repeated in succession, or knees bounces repeated in swing.

Face-to-Face Knees Bounce and Straddle Seat-Drop with Free Bounce—Partners synchronize free bounces in face-to-face position, then "A" does a straddle seat-drop, and "B" simultaneously executes a knees bounce. Both performers execute free bounces, then "B" performs a straddle seat-drop, and "A" does a knees bounce. This routine may also be performed in swing, eliminating the free bounce.

Side-by-Side, All Fundamental Bounces—All seven of the fundamental bounces may be performed singly or in routines in the side-by-side position, with both performers facing in the same direction. Side-by-side bouncing may also be performed in an alternate position, wherein the participants take position side by side, facing in opposite directions. Each performer bends his arm—the one nearest his partner—at the elbow, extends his forearm at right angles to his upper arm, and clasps the inner side of his partner's arm just above the elbow. With practice, all the fundamental bounces except the hands bounce can be executed from this alternate position.

Tandem Straddle Seat-Drop—Participants take position one behind the other, both facing in the same direction. The man in front bends his arms, bringing his forearms upward and backward. The rear man grasps his partner's forearms. When free bounces are synchronized, both participants execute straddle seat-drops in unison. The straddle seat-drop and the feet bounce with simple variations are the only exercises which can be satisfactorily performed in this position.

Face-to-Face Knees Bounce, Free Bounce, Side-by-Side-Seat-Drop—Performers synchronize bounces in the face-to face position, then both execute the knees bounce. Both then execute a free bounce in unison, shifting during the free bounce to the *alternate* side-by-side position. Upon completion of the free bounce, both execute regular seat-drops in the alternate side-by-side position.

Side-by-Side Rocking Chair—Using the *regular* side-by-side position, performers execute back-drops in swing from the feet take-off position.

Tandem Feet Bounce with Half Twist—Partners begin with simultaneous feet bounces in the tandem position. Immediately after take-off, the rear man releases his grip, and both performers execute half twists in the same direction. During the descent, the grip is re-established, and the landing is made in tandem position.

OVER-AND-UNDER BOUNCING

Certain features of the techniques employed in both alternate and simultaneous bouncing are combined in the execution of over-and-under exercises and routines, and many of the general instructions regarding safety, coordination, and teamwork cited in the two preceding sections hold true here.

Since as many as three performers may participate at one time in this form of group tumbling, bed set should be adjusted to accommodate this additional load, and to make possible the high bounces which are required for the execution of certain exercises.

In over-and-under bouncing—as the name indicates—one performer passes over the other during the course of the exercise. It will be found that the problem of timing is simplified when the performer who passes underneath is always required to time the action and adjust his movements to those of the man who passes over him.

In most exercises and routines involving over-and-under action, the man who passes over his partner must achieve a certain amount of forward or backward travel during his bounce. Normally, the top man executes his take-off from a point about one foot from the center of the bed, and lands on the opposite side at an equal distance from center.

The introduction of a third participant in some exercises and routines serves to complicate the problems of timing, control, and spotting. However, the difficulties thus presented all stem from the necessity of achieving precise teamwork and automatic coordination, and may all be overcome by practice and careful execution.

In originating over-and-under exercises and routines, certain limitations necessary to avoid interference between the performers must be accepted. The limitations thus imposed, however, offer a double challenge to the trampoline tumbler. As an indication of the possibilities present in this form of group tumbling, examples of over-and-under exercises and routines involving two and three performers are listed on the next page.

OVER-AND-UNDER EXERCISES AND ROUTINES

(Two Persons)

Straddle Over and Walk Under—Performers face each other across the center of the bed. "A" does a feet bounce in straddle position, and "B" walks under. "A" does a feet bounce with a half twist as "B" turns around, then the exercise is repeated.

Straddle Over and Roll Under—This exercise is begun in the same manner as the one above. As "A" does his straddle feet bounce, "B" executes a forward roll on the bed, passing under "A". "B" recovers and turns around while "A" does a feet bounce with a half twist, and the exercise is then repeated.

Somersault Over and Walk Under—Performers face each other. "A" executes a high forward somersault, and "B" walks under. "A" does a feet bounce with half twist, "B" turns around, and the exercise is repeated. A forward roll may be employed for variation, or a barany substituted for the forward somersault.

Somersault Over and Somersault Under—Performers start the exercise facing each other. "A" executes a high forward somersault, "B" performs a low, fast somersault, passing beneath "A".

Forward One-and-Three-Quarter Somersault to Back-Drop, Rebound Somersault to Feet, Side Roll Under—The side or shoulder roll is done under the rebound somersault.

Forward Somersault with Full Twist and Roll Under.

Barani Over and Roll Under—In this exercise, a backward somersault may be substituted for the free bounce.

Forward One-and-a-Quarter Somersault and Walk Under—Performer doing somersault should start from center of bed to give partner clearance for walk under and avoid striking him with feet on come-out.

Forward One-and-a-Quarter Somersault with Half Twist and Roll Under.

Backward Somersault Over and Walk Under—Performers take positions on opposite sides of the center of the bed, facing in the *same* direction. "A" does a high backward somersault, and "B" walks under.

Backward Somersault with Full Twist and Roll Under.

Backward One-and-a-Quarter Somersault to Back-Drop, Backover to Feet and Walk Under—"A" does one-and-a quarter backward somersault, then backover to feet. "B" walks under backover. "B" must give "A" a double-lift for backover. (See section on "Shoulder Mounts and Dismounts".)

Backward Somersault Over and Roll Under—As above, substituting roll under for walk under.

Backward Somersault Over, Roll Under, Forward Somersault Over, Roll Under—"A" does backward somersault over, and "B" rolls under. "A" does a free bounce, while "B" turns around. "A" then does a forward somersault over and "B" rolls under. Variation: After "A" does forward somersault over, he breaks and turns around. "B", having rolled under, does a free bounce, then a backward somersault over "A", who rolls under. Both continue the routine.

Backward Somersault Over, Roll Under, Free Bounce, and Reverse—"A" does a backward somersault, a free bounce, and breaks. "B" rolls under, does a free bounce, and then a backward somersault. "A" rolls under. The routine is repeated with "A" and "B" in reversed positions. Variations: Substitute full twist for free bounce following somersault. Substitute somersault with full twist for regular somersault.

(Three Persons)

Straddle Over and Walk Under—"A" faces "B" and "C", with the latter standing behind "B". "A" does two straddle bounces over "B" and "C", while they walk under one at a time. "A" then does a bounce with a half twist while "B" and "C" turn around to face "A". The exercise is repeated with "C" walking under first. Variation: "A" bounces over "B" and "C" does half twist. "B" bounces with half twist after walking under "A" and then bounces over "C" and "A" with half twist. "B" bounces with half twist after walking under "A" and then bounces over "C" and "A" with half twist. Then "C" goes through the same routine.

Straddle Over and Double Walk Under—Same as first exercise except that "B" and "C" walk under tandem style. They also may walk under side by side.

Straddle Over and Roll Under—Same as first exercise, substituting roll under for walk under.

Straddle Over and Double Roll Under—Roll is done in tandem style. Variations: Roll under side by side.

Somersault Over and Walk Under—Same as first exercise, substituting forward somersault for straddle over. Variations: Same as in first exercise

Somersault Over and Double Walk Under—Walk under in tandem style or side by side.

Somersault Over and Roll Under—Same as first exercise, substituting roll under for walk under.

Somersault Over and Double Roll Under—Same exercise as somersault over and double walk under, substituting roll under for walk under. Variation: Roll under side by side.

Straddle Bounce Over and Roll Under—"A" and "C" face each other at opposite ends of bed, while "B" in center of bed faces "A". "A" straddle bounces over "B" who does forward roll under. "A" does forward roll under "C" as "C" straddle bounces over. "C" does forward roll under "B" who has turned around in the meantime and prepared to straddle bounce over.

Somersault Over, Roll Under, Straddle Over, Roll Under—"A" does a forward somersault over "B" and straddle bounces over "C". "B" and "C" roll under. "A" bounces with half twist while "B" and "C" turn around.

Barani Over and Double Roll Under—"A" does barani over "B" and "C" who roll under side by side.

Barani Over, Roll Under, Backward Somersault Over, Roll Under—"A" does baran over "B" and backward somersault over "C" as "B" and "C" roll under. Turn and repeat as in first exercise.

SHOULDER MOUNTS AND DISMOUNTS

The ability to perform exercises and routines involving shoulder mounts and dismounts is a valuable accomplishment for the trampoline tumbler who enjoys participation in group tumbling. These skills lend themselves to a wide variety of applications, and are particularly well suited to advanced exhibition work.

The mounts employed are almost identical to those used in ground tumbling and acrobatics. When performed on the trampoline, the footing is, of course, less stable; but the action of the bed eliminates most of the lifting required when mounts are executed on the ground.

One of the most important techniques involved in the execution of shoulder mounts and dismounts is proper breaking on the part of the bottom man. In mounts which employ bounce lifts—that is, the combination of a bounce and arm-lift—the man who occupies the bottom position must break as the top man bounces prior to mounting, flexing his legs to absorb the recoil of the bed and thus avoid being thrown out of position. In bounce mounts, where no arm-lift is used, an action called the "double-lift" is often employed to enable the top man to acquire sufficient height of bounce for the mount. Here the bottom man times a short beat with his partner's take-off beat, breaking as the top man takes off and thus allowing the top man to receive the full recoil from the double beat.

In all mounts, the bottom man must flex his legs as his partner lands on his shoulders, to avoid insofar as possible the transmission of landing shock to the bed, which might result in an uncontrollable two-high bounce. In addition, the bottom man is always responsible for correct "spotting" of the mount—that is, he is charged with placing himself in correct position beneath his partner during the execution of the mount.

Various mounts and dismounts may be combined with certain basic exercises to form simple or advanced routines. On the following page, the most generally used mounts and dismounts, together with suggested routines, are listed and described.

EXERCISES AND ROUTINES WITH MOUNTS AND DISMOUNTS

Forward Bounce-Lift to Front Mount—Partners face each other and take wrist-lock grip. Top man bounces up and slightly forward, legs apart. Bottom man lifts and guides partner into position. Grip is broken as top man's feet land on partner's shoulders. Bottom man grasps top man's legs—top man straightens to erect position.

Backward Bounce-Lift to Back Mount—Partners face in same direction, bottom man behind top man. Hands are clasped in lock-grip. Top man bounces up; partner lifts and guides him into position. Grip is released, and bottom man grasps top man's legs above calves, pulling legs tight against head for firm support.

Cross-Arms Bounce-Lift to Back Mount—Performers stand face-to-face. Right hands are clasped as in shaking hands. Left hands are clasped above right hands, arms rotated outward, thumbs down, and palms facing performer's left. As top man bounces upward, bottom man lifts him and swings him around over shoulder to back mount. Grip is released, and legs are grasped as described above.

Forward Bounce to Front Mount—From face-to-face position, top man bounces up and slightly forward, landing on his partner's shoulders. Bottom man grasps top man's legs as landing is made.

Backward Bounce to Back Mount—Bottom man stands behind top man, both facing in the same direction. Top man bounces straight up. Bottom man steps forward and receives top man on his shoulders, grasping top man's legs as landing is made.

Backward Bounce, Half Twist to Front Mount—Body must be kept erect. Bounce straight upward as twist is made.

Forward Bounce, Half Twist to Back Mount—Twist is done with feet apart. Bounce must be high enough to give bottom man time to spot partner as twist is completed.

Dismounts: 1. Forward Dismount: Top man dismounts forward from a front or back mount. Arm lifts are not employed. Top man flexes legs slightly as bottom man works the bed; bottom man releases grip on partner's legs as top man takes off. Top man lands behind bottom man from front mount, and in front of bottom man from back mount. Bottom man times beat slowly. Variations: Dismount to front-drop, or turnover to back-drop. Dismount with half twist to feet or back-drop. 2. Backward Dismount: Top man dismounts backward from front or back mount. Variations: Dismount to back-drop or seat-drop. Dismount with half twist to feet or front-drop. Dismount with full twist to back-drop.

Forward Bounce-Lift to Front Mount, Backward Dismount, Repeat in Swing—Mount is executed as previously described. Wrist-lock grip is resumed during dismount, and top man mounts again as he rebounds from dismount.

Forward Bounce to Front Mount, Backward Dismount, Repeat in Swing—From face-to-face position, top man bounces up, landing on partner's shoulders. After backward dismount top man mounts again as he rebounds from dismount. Variations: Same exercise with somersault or full twist following dismount.

Forward Bounce to Front Mount, Backward Dismount with Half Twist, Backward Bounce to Back Mount—Top man bounces up and forward to partner's shoulders, then executes a backward dismount with half twist. As top man rebounds from dismount, partner steps forward and top man lands on bottom man's shoulders.

Forward Bounce to Front Mount, Backward Dismount with Half Twist, Bounce with Half Twist to Front Mount, Repeat in Swing—Same as preceding exercise. After dismount, top man again bounces up with half twist to front mount.

Bounce-Lift to Back Mount, Forward Dismount, Repeat in Swing—Bounce-lift to back mount as previously described. Top man executes forward dismount. Variations: Same with somersault or full twist following dismount.

Backward Bounce-Lift to Back Mount Retaining Hand Lock Grasp, Forward Dismount, Lift-Away Somersault in Hands— Partners face in same direction, bottom man behind top man. Hands are clasped in lock-grip. Top man bounces up while partner retains lock-grip. Top man dismounts forward between arms of partner. On rebound from dismount top man does forward somersault as partner lifts. Variations: Grip may be released as somersault is executed and come-out is made. (Somersault should be tucked to avoid hitting bottom man with feet.) Same exercise with half twisting somersault or barany. Lock-grip may be released early.

Forward Somersault, Bounce to Front Mount—Variation: Barany, bounce to back mount.

Backward Somersault, Backward Bounce to Back Mount.

Back Mount, Forward Dismount, Bounce-Lift to High Hand-to-Hand—Variations: Partners may clasp hands before dismount or during bounce.

Backward Somersault to Back Mount—Top man must bounce high and turn fast for come-out on shoulders. Partner (whose head should be well protected) watches top man's center of rotation and gets directly under it for catch. Variations: Exercise may also be started from back mount to forward dismount.

Back-Drop, Backover to Back Mount—"A" stands in front of "B", both facing in same direction. "A" does back-drop, then backover. "B" gives "A" a double-lift for the backover, enabling "A" to attain sufficient height for the back mount. For variation, the backover may be done to a sitting position on "B's" hands, instead of to back mount. To accomplish this, "A" must pike to sitting position prior to landing on "B's" hands and maintain this position rigidly to facilitate the balancing of his weight by "B". It is important that "A" complete the backover with his head bent well forward, to lessen the danger of striking "B" with his head. "B", through practice, will discover the point of balance for his "catch", usually on the back of the thighs rather than on the buttocks. Gripping the "hamstring" muscles to steady the catch is helpful. The catch may be practiced by having "A" bounce from feet into position on "B's" hands. This variation is easier to accomplish than the back mount to the shoulders.

Backward One-and-a-Quarter Somersault, Backover to Back Mount—Same as preceding exercise, except that one-and-a-quarter somersault is substituted for the back-drop. May also be done to sitting position on bottom man's hands.

Back-Drop, Bounce to Front Mount—Use regular back-drop beat, and take off with some turnover motion. Flex legs after take-off. Variation: Same exercise to hands of bottom man.

11

Exhibitions

The organization and presentation of exhibitions provide the instructor with outstanding opportunities for the stimulation of enthusiastic participation and the encouragement of creative endeavor. Suggestions as to the nature and scope of these demonstrations are contained in the following paragraphs.

Trampoline tumbling lends itself more readily to the presentation of exhibitions than does any other gymnastic activity. The problems involved in moving, setting up, and dismantling equipment are minimized—for the trampoline is light, compact, and easy to move and erect. A single trampoline may be used for all age groups, and the wide variety of exercises which may be performed makes possible a diversified program without the tedious delays involved in rearrangement of apparatus or introduction of additional equipment. Moreover, audience appeal is assured, for no form of athletics is more spectacular or attention-compelling than advanced trampoline tumbling.

Many opportunities for the staging of exhibitions present themselves throughout the school year. Parent-teacher meetings, assemblies, class days, school circuses—all are appropriate occasions for the demonstration of individual or class skills. Moreover, since trampoline tumbling requires but a single piece of apparatus which is easily moved, short exhibitions have proved extremely popular as between-the-halves entertainment at football and basketball games.

Exhibitions may be held indoors or out of doors, and any number of performers—both boys and girls of all age groups—may participate. The exhibition may consist of individual exercises and routines, group tumbling, or any combination of these skills. Any program can be made entertaining and impressive if presented in a confident manner in a planned sequence which avoids delay and duplication.

Even the simplest exercises may be presented effectively if good showmanship is employed. In this connection, it is the author's conviction that comedy adds much to any exhibition of trampoline tumbling. Both are, in a way, inseparable. There are many opportunities for injecting laugh-provoking antics into the sequence of routines. Particularly the element of falling—the never-failing standby of comedy—will provide situations on the trampoline which are sure to hold the interests of the spectators and to draw laughs. Many legitimate exercises may be made to change their character by accentuating or exaggerating certain movements. The personal characteristics of the performer, too, are a factor in attaining the purpose of entertaining the spectators. Almost any routine may be burlesqued for the comic effect.

This light touch given to trampoline tumbling performances is an excellent means for putting both spectators and performers at ease. It promotes confidence and initiative as well as interest and relaxation. Finally, it gives many a performer a chance to display and perfect natural aptitudes for comedy which otherwise might not have come to light. Comedy, therefore, should never be omitted entirely, for it always creates a comfortable atmosphere which is invariably reflected in a more confident and natural performance.

Most important of all, however, the exhibition provides

outstanding opportunities for the development and functioning of initiative and creative capacity on the part of both instructors and students—a factor of prime importance which cannot be disregarded in any educational process.

The following sample is presented as a suggested trampoline comedy routine for three performers:

Suggested music: Medley of waltzes—such as "Meet Me in St. Louis, Louis," "Coming Through the Rye," "Humoresque," "The Band Played On," and "School Days" —set to tempo of bouncing. Introduction and finish routine require fast gallops.

The performers, "A", "B" and "C", run out on stage to the trampoline, one behind the other. "A" is in the lead, and falls down on stage just before reaching the trampoline. "B" and "C" step on him as they mount the trampoline. "B" proceeds to end of bed and turns to face "C". They start alternate bouncing and go into teeter-totter routine. They finish by jumping off the trampoline, facing audience. Side by side, they jump off the trampoline *frame*—not the bed.

By the time they dismount, "A" is up on the trampoline and does his first individual routine—simple comedy variations, dives, etc. Safety considerations permitting, he "mugs" toward the audience throughout routine. Having finished his routine, he takes elaborate bow, but stays on bed while "B" appears and starts bouncing. "A" walks under "B" on his third bounce ("B" should count "one, two," etc., so "A" will not be confused about timing the walk under). In other words, they do the straddle-over-walk-under routine. This must be practiced so that "B" does not travel from one end of the bed to the other, but just over center, while "A" travels under him. Next, a comic variation of this routine is introduced—the spectator receives the impression that "A" is knocked down, whereas actually he falls down at exactly the moment he comes in contact with his partner. The variation is performed in the following manner—on the third walk-under, "A" looks up at "B", gestures for him to stop—calling out, "wait a minute," as though he expects "B" to stop in mid-air—and then takes the knock-down. "A" pretends that he is mad at "B", and gets off the trampoline. In learning the straddle-on-neck knock-down, "A" should walk well under "B" and lean backward at the same time. "A" actually falls backward—he is not knocked off balance, as it appears. He immediately rebounds from the back-drop to his feet. It is good comedy to learn this well enough so that "A" can "mug" toward the audience as he walks under, without looking at "B".

At the completion of the knock-down routine, "B" stays on and does his first single routine. While he dismounts, "C" gets on and does his first single routine. "A" runs to jump on the trampoline, but his foot gets entangled in the springs (leg deep) over the end railing. Finally extricating himself, he gets on the trampoline. By this time, "B" is back on the trampoline with the skipping-rope, and hands one end of it to "A". They do the rope-skipping routine, with "C" skipping while "A" and "B" turn the rope. (Music: School Days.) "C" does fundamental variations. He then takes "B's" end of the rope and turns while "B" skips. Then "A" takes his turn at the skipping.[1] He does one seat-drop, one front-drop, and then stands up and does straight bouncing, while "B" and "C" give him "hot pepper". This requires "A" to flex his

[1] In rope skipping, the turners are responsible for the timing and for keeping the rope clear of both the performer (skipper) and the trampoline frame. The bed must be hit each time with the rope. It takes practice to learn to control a change of pace for low and high tricks. The skipper should not have to watch the rope at all. Start turning under skipper after he has started bouncing—not over him. One turner should give the other a signal for starting the turning.

knees sharply, lifting his feet off bed very fast in tempo with the turning of the rope. He does not bounce, but simply does a series of "breaks" in fast tempo. He finally gets caught by the rope at his ankles, falls down, and gets off the trampoline fast. "B" and "C" stay on and each does an advanced routine.

The three performers then assemble on the trampoline for finish routine: the straddle-over roll-under.[2] A basic requirement for the success of this routine is a thorough mastery of the straddle-over walk-under. The performance is finished with all three stepping off the trampoline simultaneously, side by side, for a bow. (Music: fast gallop.)

[2] Learn to roll under without bouncing. Be sure to keep head downward and forward throughout roll and start from center of bed. Roll must be done fairly fast, but not rushed; and measured for distance, so performer will not finish the roll over the springs.

12

Competition

Trampoline, as a competitive event, first received national recognition when introduced as a special event in the National AAU Gymnastics Championships at Dallas, Texas in 1947. The following year the NCAA included the trampoline in their gymnastics competition, and since that time the trampoline has become a competitive sport throughout the world. The sport received its early development in the United States as part of the gymnastics program. However, in other countries where gymnastics was steeped in tradition, the trampoline has developed as a separate sport. This separation from gymnastics has now occurred in the United States as well, and competition in the sport is sponsored by the AAU; the NCAA; the United States Gymnastics Federation, a professional trampoline association; and by other national organizations such as the YMCAs. Rules bodies, such as the NCAA gymnastics rules committee and study committees of coaches associations in the United States, have provided the rest of the world with leadership for the development of competitive rules. However, the International Federation of Trampoline (FIT) has been formed to govern competition between two or more countries, and the rules of the FIT are determined by delegates of the member countries. FIT rules represent a long evolution of trampoline competition and in any new program these rules should probably be used with modifications to fit the particular situation and age group of the competitors.

HISTORY OF TRAMPOLINE COMPETITION

In the earliest competitions, the performers were allowed a time limit of from one minute to one minute 30 seconds, and later from 45 seconds to one minute, in which to complete the competitive routine. The meets were virtually endurance contests and the routines included many intermediate bounces and almost no continuity. To encourage more continuity in the routine and to shorten the time required to administer the event, procedures were changed to allow each performer three sequences of eight contacts with the bed and 10 seconds rest between each sequence. Along with this change came the concept of continuous swing-time routines with a logical beginning and ending. In 1958 the complaint that the third sequence was merely a repetition of the first two caused the NCAA and the AAU to adopt two sequences of 10 contacts with a 20 second rest between them as the standard routine. The length of this routine seemed too long for safety, and therefore, in 1959 the two organizations shortened the standard exercise to two sequences with eight contacts.

So, while the trampoline was part of a gymnastics competition, it was being administered differently from the other events in the sport of gymnastics. In other events the gymnast was allowed to compose his competitive routine in any way that he saw fit so long as it met certain requirements of composition and difficulty. Therefore, the rules committee of the NCAA first moved to one sequence of from 10 to 12 contacts with the trampoline, and then later finally removed the last vestige of the old required number of contacts. During the period from 1966 to 1968 the trampoline was treated as just another event in the gymnastics meet. The tables of difficulty conformed to those used in gymnastics, the language used to describe the elements to be included in an exercise was the same, and the judging system for making deductions from 10.0 points was the same. During this period of time, a World Championship Competition was organized and financed by a manufacturer of trampolines, and at a meeting in conjunction with this competition leaders from the various countries agreed to form the FIT. Since trampoline was separate from gymnastics in most countries, the international rules were somewhat different from those used in the U.S. The international group began with the swing-time concept already well developed, and their main concern was with the development of a system of evaluation which would be fair for all. They had two models to work from, that of diving competition where the difficulty of each dive is combined with the execution score, and that of gymnastics where deductions are made, from a perfect score of 10, for flaws in the execution of the skills or for the lack of difficulty. The FIT used parts of both systems, and the final result is consistent with the nature of trampoline.

The basic form of the FIT system of competition is derived from a concept for determining difficulty called axial rotation (AR) suggested by Mr. Robert Bollinger in the United States. Mr. Bollinger's system awarded one point for each 1/4 rotation on the lateral axis and one point for each 1/2 rotation on the longitudinal axis. Under this system a double forward somersault was worth 8 points (4 points for each somersault) and a double twisting backward somersault was also worth 8 points (4 points for somersault and 4 points for the 2 twists). The following is the FIT system of competition. It is similar to the earlier American types which were based upon a gymnastics competitive model, but in a sophisticated manner it includes the work of Mr. Bollinger.

CURRENT INTERNATIONAL RULES

In FIT competition the performer is allowed exactly 10 contacts with the trampoline. He or she may take as many preparatory bounces as needed, and the counting is begun after the first stunt. After the tenth contact the performer must demonstrate a controlled bounce and a stop. Four judges are responsible for evaluating the execution of the trampolinist. A perfect score for execution is 10.0 points, and deductions are made from this in tenths of a point for imperfections in the routine. Typical imperfections are excessive traveling during the performance or poor positioning of the body and limbs during flight. Another judge is responsible for determining the difficulty of the component parts of the routine. He does this by awarding one tenth of a point for each 1/4 somersault or 1/2 twist. The difficulty judge records each stunt and its value and then adds together the values. The final score for a given performance is the total of the execution evaluation and the difficulty score.

Example:

	Position	Stunt	Value
*1.	Piked	Double Back	.9
2.	Free	Barani Out Fliffes	.9
3.	Free	Double Twisting Back	.8
4.	Tucked	Back	.4
5.	Free	Rudolph	.7
6.	Free	Full Twisting Back	.6
7.	Tucked	Double Back	.8
*8.	Piked	Back	.5
9.	Tucked	1 3/4 Back Somersault to Stomach	.7
10.	Tucked	2 1/4 Back to Feet (Double Cody)	.9
		TOTAL VALUE FOR DIFFICULTY	7.2
		EXECUTION SCORE	8.6
		FINAL SCORE	15.8

*Note: Certain skills are awarded more points than their AR would indicate due to problems of position or landing. For a complete listing you are referred to the FIT table in Chapter 8.

In international contests the trampolinists are required to perform what is called a compulsory routine. This routine is made up of trampoline maneuvers that sample the various movement possibilities of the trampoline, such as body bounces, somersaulting, and twisting. The judging of this compulsory routine is based entirely upon the execution, since the difficulty is the same for all competitors. After performing the compulsory routine the trampolinists are asked to perform their first optional routine. The scores of the compulsory and the first optional routine are then added together to determine the 10 finalists. Those who reach the finals must then complete a second optional routine which may be the same or different from the one performed earlier. The champion is the one with the highest total for all three routines. In addition to having good execution and a high degree of difficulty, the champion trampolinist in international competition must have consistency of performance. The following are International rules for trampoline competition:

1. International Trampoline competitions shall consist of one compulsory and one optional routine. The ten best participants shall be admitted to the final and in the final they have to perform their optional routine once more.
2. The starting order of the competitors will be decided by a draw. This starting order applies only for the compulsory exercises. The ranking position based on the results of the compulsory routines will decide the starting order for the optional routines. The competitor with the lowest marks starts first. There has to be a break between the compulsory and optional routines.
3. The compulsory and optional routines shall consist of 10 movements as published in the official announcements.

4. The compulsory and optional routines cannot be repeated.
5. Repetitions of one and the same jump in free exercises is not permitted. For exceptions, see points 33 e, f, and g.
6. The referee and assistant referee shall determine the difficulty values of the optional routines.
7. All jumps are named and difficulty graded in a tariff table (see Chapter 8).
8. All routines shall be performed un-aided and only the official spotters shall be allowed to stand around the Trampoline.
9. The jury consists of: one referee, one assistant referee, four judges, one counter, one recorder.
10. The jury members for international competitions must be approved by the FIT.
11. The referee shall only vote when a disagreement is involved (see Nos. 17, 24, 26).
12. The umpires must be seated next to each other on *elevated seats* at a distance of approximately 5 m (16.4 ft.) from the trampoline.
13. Trampoline routines shall be marked by tenths of points.
14. The number of points gained by a competitor shall be the total of the marks gained for "performance" plus the "tariff value."
15. The judges shall mark the performance publicly and independently by using marking cards that must be simultaneously displayed immediately on the referee's signal.
16. The judges mark only the "performance" of a routine up to 10 points.
17. When one judge fails to display his marks simultaneously with the other judges, then an average mark of

the other judges will be taken as the value for the exercise. The decision about this will be made by the referee.

18. The difficulty value for the optional routine is the total sum of the difficulty marks for each jump performed in the routine.
19. The jury should do some trial scoring in advance of the actual competition.
20. The counter aids the referee and counts each contact with the bed after first movement of the routine, as follows: 1, 2, 3–9, 10, out.
21. The recorder makes a note of the marks awarded, crosses out the highest and the lowest, and takes the average of the remaining two marks. He then adds the degree of difficulty to the performance marks, makes deductions as indicated by the referee, and records the final score for the routine.
22. The judges shall assess performance from the following points of view: a) form, b) execution, c) control.
23. The umpire deducts points for following faults: a) for posture fault, insecurity, and insufficient height of jump during each exercise part—0.1 to 0.5 points b) for insecurity after the tenth jump—0.1 to 1.0 points.
24. If the difference between the two middle performance marks given by the judges is more than 0.5 points, a special discussion by the jury shall follow.
25. The judges will make the following deductions for faulty performance

for each part of the routine

a) lack of form	0.1 to 0.5 points

and once only for the routine as a whole

b) poor execution (height, arrangement, rhythm)	0.1 to 0.5
c) lack of control (safety)	0.1 to 1.0

26. If the competitor touches with any part of his body

the frame or the suspension system, he shall be scored only on the basis of the number of skills (routine parts) he has completed up to that time.

27. If the competitor falls off the Trampoline or must be held on by the spotters, his score shall be zero points.
28. If the contestant does not execute the *obligatory exercise* in the prescribed exercise sequence and with the prescribed jumps, then the exercise is considered as having been discontinued as soon as the contestant changes it. (See also Point 29.)
29. If a competitor interrupts or stops his exercise the judges will mark him for the executed movements only (i. e. six movements completed = maximum 6 points). The referee will decide the difficulty mark up to that time. An interruption must be considered as having taken place if the resilience of the jumping sheet is not used for the immediate jump-off for the next jump thus resulting in a pause.
30. With the landing *on feet* after the tenth part of exercise (jump) the exercise is completed. The contestant is permitted, however, to add a stretched-foot jump (after-jump). If the contestant does not land on his feet after the tenth jump, then the umpire may deduct between 0.1 and 1.0 point, dependent on the extent of insecurity.
31. Additional rules for Synchronized Trampolining:
    (a) In synchronous competitions a 10 part exercise must be executed.
    (b) The trampolines must be placed parallel, next to each other at a distance between them of approximately 2 m (6.6 ft.).
    (c) The contestants begin from a starting position at an identical line of sight.
    (d) The contestants must execute the same jump (exercise part) at the same time and in the same rhythm.

(e) If one of the partners changes the sequence of jumps, then the synchronous exercise is considered as having been ended.
In such a case the degrees of difficulty are to be credited only for such jumps that have been executed by both jumpers synchronously. This rule is also applicable if both contestants, despite the faulty execution, continue the exercise up to the tenth jump.

(f) Evaluation procedure for synchronous exercises:
The competition supervisor and his assistant shall check the uniformity of jumps and determine the degree of difficulty.
Umpires 1 and 2 evaluate the form at trampoline No. 1.
Umpires 3 and 4 evaluate the form at trampoline No. 2.
The average mark for the form is calculated in the same manner as that of single competitions.
Umpires 5 and 6 (synchronous execution umpires) judge, independent of each other, the synchronous execution of the exercise and deduct points in the case of non-uniform landing:
Landing differences up to approximately 50 cm/ 1.6 ft./ 0.1 to 0.3
Landing differences in excess of 50 cm/ 1.6 ft./ 0.4 to 0.5
The mean value of both umpire marks represents the deduction of points for faulty sychronous execution.

32. Performance Regulations:
(a) He shall start on the signal given by the referee.
(b) The competitor takes as many preliminary jumps as he desires before commencing the first movement of his routine.

(c) The legs shall be closed after leaving the bed and shall remain in this stretched position while the performer is in the air.

(d) The legs have to be properly stretched, tucked, or piked, as the case may be for each movement.

(e) In the tucked position, the body should be rolled up closely with the knees tight together. The hands grasp the legs below the knees.

(f) For combination movements (somersaults with twists) the competitor himself may decide in which phase he will perform the twist, if the table in degree of difficulty does not warrant otherwise.

(g) Fliffis may, although being the same skill, be performed in different ways. These skills are classed as different tricks but still have the same difficulty rating.

33. Explanations of the table on degree of difficulty:

(a) The difficulty grades in this table (1-15) are in tenths of points.

(b) The degree of difficulty for every jump is worked out on the following principle:

Quarter of a somersault (90 degrees)	= 1 tenth of a point
Somersault (360 degrees)	= 4 tenths of a point
Half Twist (180 degrees)	= 1 tenth of a point
Full Twist (360 degrees)	= 2 tenths of a point

(c) Pike and stretched (layout) jumps receive, if turns are 360° or more, an additional one tenth of a point, provided they are executed without simultaneous twists.

(d) Backward one-and-three-quarter and two-and-three-quarter somersaults gain respectively .9 points and 1.3 points.

(e) Tucked, piked, and layout jumps are considered as different jumps and not as repetitions.

(f) The same goes for the twists and multiple somersaults.

(g) Double somersaults with a half twist in the first, middle, or last phase have the same degree of difficulty, but are considered to be different jumps.

34. Assistance. During each contest 4 assistants who are appointed by the organizer must stand at the trampoline. They must be fully prepared for the carrying out of their task.

35. Each umpire must have a person assigned to him for taking down, in writing, point deductions.

36. Sportswear for Contest. Men: sportshirt, sportshorts, trampoline shoes. Women: gymnastic tights, trampoline shoes.

37. Repeat of Exercise. The umpires may order, by a majority decision, the repeat of an exercise, should a contestant be obviously impeded during the execution of the exercise. e.g.: trampoline material defect, upset of contestant by lighting or spectators.

38. In all contests the number of points determined for an exercise must be made known before the next contestant enters the trampoline.

39. Contest chart. All contestants must enter the intended free exercise on the contest chart and submit it one hour prior to the contest start. A change of the jump sequence during the execution of the exercise is permitted, however.

PLANNING AND CONDUCTING A TRAMPOLINE COMPETITION

Trampoline competition consists of a session in which all competitors complete the required routine for the meet, another session for each competitor to demonstrate his optional routine, and a final session in which the ten best competitors compete for final placings. Administering a meet of this type is not difficult, but in order to have a smooth presentation the host should carefully plan the minute details regarding forms, personnel, and equipment needed. Even the best planning will leave last minute items that will need attention, but these things should be kept to a minimum. Another reason for advanced planning is consideration of the way in which you will present trampoline competition to the spectators, participants, and the officials. As the host you are the leader in presenting the sport, and the way that you treat trampolining will be the way that others believe to be the correct way. There are some rather obvious items to consider such as selecting a date and site, and notifying or advertising for the participants. Beyond these items are a few basic ones given below in brief form. One can easily peruse this list and determine which items must be dealt with long before the meet starts, and those that can wait until the day of the competition. However, your planning should culminate with these things accounted for before the meet begins. Depending upon the magnitude of the competition you may find other aspects such as concessions, selling advertisements for the program, etc., which you may care to add to this list.

EQUIPMENT AND MATERIALS NECESSARY

1. Trampoline.
2. Score table, score sheets, rule book.
3. Public address system and script for the announcer.
4. Four raised chairs for the judges, and 12 chairs for the other officials in the competition.
5. Flash cards for the judges assistants.

6. Tickets, medals for the winners, programs.
7. Forms for scoring, Figures 3 and 4; for reporting routines before the meet, Figure 2; for recording the value of the routines as they are performed, Figure 2; for each judge's score, Figure 1.
8. A detailed floor plan showing the placement of the equipment and how the space will be decorated.

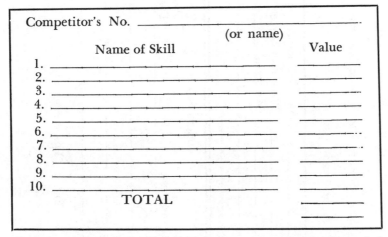

Judge's Number ______________________________
Competitor's No. ______________________________
(or name)
Score Given ______________________________

Four are needed for each routine. They can be color coded to make identification and scoring more accurate.

Fig. 1

Competitor's No. ______________________________
(or name)

Name of Skill	Value
1. ______________________	________
2. ______________________	________
3. ______________________	________
4. ______________________	________
5. ______________________	________
6. ______________________	________
7. ______________________	________
8. ______________________	________
9. ______________________	________
10. ______________________	________
TOTAL	________

One is needed by each participant to report the intended routine before the meet, and one is needed by the difficulty judge, as he records the skills and values while the routine is actually being performed.

Fig. 2

Score Sheets (Use A Ditto Master)

A. For Each Session

Session ______________ Name of Competition ____________________ Date____________
Scorer __________________ Place of Competition ___________________________________
Referee _________________ Assistant ___________________ Superior Judge _____________
Judges 1. ______________ 2. ______________ 3. _________________ 4. _______________
Counter _________________

Name-Organization	Judges Scores 1	2	3	4	Total For Form	Diff Value	Final Mark	Place
1.								
2.								
3.								

Fig. 3 (Three Needed)

B. Summary Score Sheet

Attendance ____________

Arizona Invitational
University of Arizona
Tucson, Arizona

October 6, 1968

Officials: Referee ____________ Assistant ____________
Superior Judge ____________ Scorer ____________ Counter ____________
Judges: 1. ____________ 2. ____________ 3. ____________ 4. ____________

Name	Organization	Score For First Opt		Running Total Score Final Session		Total	Place
		D	E	D	E		
1.							
2.							
3.							

Figure 4 (One Needed)

PERSONNEL NEEDED FOR THE COMPETITION

1. The director of the competition.
2. Referee and assistant referee.
3. Four judges and four assistants for the judges.
4. One counter.
5. One superior official.
6. Four official spotters.
7. Scoring personnel (two or three).
8. Announcer. (Choose this person carefully for he is extremely important to a smooth competition.)

DESCRIPTION OF A COMPETITION

Opening Ceremony—The arrangements have been made, the field of competitors is filled, and the advance publicity arrangements indicate that a fine crowd is expected for the competition which will begin at 8:00 p.m. The meet director and his assistants have been very busy, and the equipment is set on the floor by 6:00 P.M. Everything is in readiness. The competitors arrive, report their intended routines, dress, and begin to warm up. Light background music plays while the spectators arrive. Finally, with ten minutes to go before the start of the competition the officials of the meet take their places, and the competitors are asked to conclude their warm ups. Last minute details are checked before the announcer welcomes the spectators and introduces the competitors who line up facing the audience. Everyone rises while the national anthem is played. While the spectators take their seats the officials of the competition are introduced, and then the first competitor is called.

The Competition—Each competitor completes his routine as the official counter calls aloud each contact with the bed (ten are allowed). During the routine the referee identifies each skill as it is performed, and his assistant records the skill and its value. When the routine is concluded the assistant referee adds together all of the values to determine the total mark for difficulty. Also, as the trampolinist performs, the four judges are marking down deductions for faults in the execution and form of each skill. The scores of the four judges, and the score of the referee is carried to the score table for tabulation. The scoring table computes the score in the following manner: the highest score and the lowest score of the four judges are eliminated, and the two middle scores are added together and averaged to determine the final score for execution. The score for execution and the score given by the referee for difficulty are added together to determine the final mark given for a routine. (See example in the section concerned with rules.) The scoring process must be completed before the next competitor may begin, and the announcer calls up the next performer during this time. He also gives the spectators information regarding the rules, and items that may be of interest to them. It is an especially good idea for him to aquaint the people with information about the sport, since it is still young and the fundamentals of competition are not common knowledge.

Following each session there is usually allowed a short time for the competitors in the next session to warm up again. This time is kept to a minimum, and throughout this period the results of the competition up to this time are read while background music is played.

After The Competition—When the last trampolinist completes his routine the scores must be computed for his performance, but the music begins and the victory stand is moved into place for the presentations to the winners. After the presentations of the medals, the audience moves out while background music plays. However, the task of the competition's organizers is still not ended. The scores must be rechecked and the final results of the meet must be disseminated to the judges, competitors, interested spectators, and press. The results should also be telephoned to the local newspapers, radio and television stations.

AGE GROUP TRAMPOLINE COMPETITION

Currently, there is no national age group program for trampoline competition, but if higher and higher levels of perfection are to be reached, the age at which children begin to learn the fundamentals of bouncing and competition must be lowered and a national program produced. An age group program introduces many youngsters to the fine activity of bouncing, and it identifies at an early age those who have talent and a love for the sport. In the following paragraphs are a few concepts relative to the forming of an age group program at the local level. From the efforts of those attempting local programs will grow the interest and the leadership needed to produce a national program.

A developmental program for children must be based upon concepts that will insure the successful participation of all who are involved. The first of these concepts is surely safety. A child may attempt more than his capability might suggest as safe, if he is allowed to choose the skills that he will present in a competition. They may also skip those fundamentals they find difficult and overuse those they find easy to learn. Also, difficulty is especially intriguing to a very young trampolinist, and it is suggested that a series of progressively more difficult compulsory routines be used for competition among youngsters. Five of these routines would probably be enough for a start, and in each an emphasis should be placed upon fundamental work leading to the development of good technique in somersaulting, twisting, ball-out, and cody work. A simple rule to use is "A performer may not compete using the second compulsory routine until the first one has been used with sureness in a competition." The routines selected may be composed especially for the local program, or routines given in Chapter 9 may be used.

A second concept that must be considered in an age group program is fairness. One cannot ask an 8 year old boy to compete against a boy of 12. The difference in maturity and strength is too great. The boys and girls should have very definite age limits within which they compete. The best arrangement would be to have everyone competing against others of the same maturational level, but this is too bulky and too difficult for easy administration. Therefore, it is recommended that an age breakdown be used similar to the swimming program. This scheme allows for five age groups that are easy to administer. The age groups are as follows: 8 years of age and under, 9 and 10 year olds, 11 and 12 year olds, 13 and 14 year olds, and 15 to 17 years of age. The first two age groups will correspond roughly to the elementary school years, the next two to the junior high school years, and the last to the high school.

A competitive unit or team can be formed by anyone who has a trampoline in his backyard, or by an organization with a trampoline available. The main ingredient is leadership, for with any large group of youngsters a responsible person must take charge. The leader must arrange for practice times, supervise and instruct during the practices, arrange the competitive schedule with other teams, and serve as a liaison between teams and parents. If at all possible, it is desirable for the leader of the team to receive some sort of financial assistance, since this will place the position of leadership on a more professional basis. Finances may be easy for a club to find, but in the case of the backyard team each participant may be charged a fee for instruction and for the administration of the program.

Competition for teams and individuals may be of several types. The people interested in starting an age group trampoline program must make a policy decision in this regard before the season of competition begins. The first type is to form teams with three boys and three girls in each age bracket. These teams would compete against other similar teams in what are called "dual meets." The boys compete against the boys and the girls compete against the girls, and points are awarded to the team on the basis of their finish (6 for first, 5 for second, etc.). The team at the end of the competition with the most accumulated points for all the age groups would be the winning team. However, all participants should receive a ribbon signifying the place that he earned. Several of these teams may form a league, and the members of the league determine the length of the season. After a series of dual meets, the league holds a championship meet with all participants being able to demonstrate their skill against all other teams at the same time.

The second type of competitive organization is to call together the leaders of the various participating groups in the beginning of the program for the purpose of setting dates on which championship tournaments will be held. Three to five of these tournaments in a summer program are appropriate. In each of these tournaments interested trampolinists compete against all others in the same age group. The concept of increasingly more difficult compulsory routines is an important one for this type of competition since the emotional quality of a championship meet is always higher than for a meet between two teams. This second type of competitive organization is very effective, and small clubs are not penalized for fielding an incomplete team. In these championship tournaments the numbers of awards should be quite high. The youngsters are sensitive, and for many this may be the last opportunity they have to win an award in an athletic endeavor.

Finally, a constant problem in any trampoline competition is securing qualified officials. In an age group program this problem is an especially serious one. When the leaders of the program decide upon the required routines to be used for competition, the value of each exercise should be precisely designated, and only a few important and common errors should be selected for the judges to notice. Once this is done, it is a very simple matter to teach interested people and parents how to evaluate the routines in the age group situation. By giving them the values of the several routines and by controlling the number of errors that they notice, fair judging is possible with a minimum of training. Above all, the system chosen must be fair for the participants, and people without training should not be asked to evaluate complex maneuvers for form and difficulty. In effect, when selecting the errors to be noticed by the officials, the habit patterns of both the officials, the coaches, and the participants are formed. The errors selected are those that the coaches will seek to overcome in their practice periods. As the program becomes more complex, evaluation may also advance.

Trampoline Champions
World Amateur

Men	Women
1964 Danny Millman, USA	1964 Judy Wills, USA
1965 Gary Erwin, USA	1965 Judy Wills, USA
1966 Wayne Miller, USA	1966 Judy Wills, USA
1967 David Jacobs, USA	1967 Judy Wills, USA
1968 David Jacobs, USA	1968 Judy Wills, USA

Synchronized Pairs

Men		Women	
1966	W. Miller & D. Jacobs, USA	1966	J. Wills & N. Smith, USA
1967	K. Treiten & H. Riehle, W. Germany	1967	J. Wills & N. Smith, USA
1968	M. Budenburg & C. Foerster, W. Germany	1968	U. Czech & A. Jaroch, W. Germany

World Professional Champions
1966 George Hery, USA
1967 Gary Erwin, USA

NCAA National Champions
(There is no women's competition in NCAA)

1948 Gay Hughes, Univ. of Illinois
1949 Edsel Buchanan, Univ. of Michigan
1950 Edsel Buchanan, Univ. of Michigan
1951 Edsel Buchanan, Univ. of Michigan
1952 Dick Gutting, Florida State Univ.
1953 Bob Hazlett, Univ. of Iowa
1954 James Norman, Univ. of Iowa
1955 Dick Albershardt, Indiana Univ.
1956 Don Harper, Ohio State Univ.
1957 Glenn Wilson, Western Illinois State
1958 Don Harper, Ohio State Univ.
1959 Ed Cole, Univ. of Michigan
1960 Larry Snyder, Univ. of Iowa
1961 Tom Gompf, Ohio State Univ.
1962 Steve Johnson, Michigan State Univ.
1963 Gary Erwin, Univ. of Michigan

1964 Gary Erwin, Univ. of Michigan
1965 Frank Schmitz, Southern Illinois Univ.
1966 Wayne Miller, Univ. of Michigan
1967 David Jacobs, Univ. of Michigan
1968 George Huntzicker, Univ. of Michigan
1969 David Jacobs, Univ. of Michigan
1970 George Huntzicker, Univ. of Michigan

AAU—Men

1947 James Garner, Los Angeles, Unattached
1948 Robert Schoendube, Univ. of Michigan
1949 Edsel Buchanan, Unattached
1950 Not held
1951 Not held
1952 Frank LaDue, Univ. of Iowa
1953 Dick Gutting, Florida State Gymkana
1954 Robert Elliot, Maverick Boys' Club, Amarillo, Texas
1955 Robert Elliot, Maverick Boys' Club, Amarillo, Texas
1956 Ronald Munn, Nard's Trampoline Club, Amarillo, Tex.
1957 Jeffrey Austin, Naval Air Base, Pensacola, Florida
1958 Glenn Wilson, Western Illinois State
1959 Ronald Munn, Unattached
1960 Larry Snyder, Univ. of Iowa
1961 Tom Osterlund, Univ. of Michigan
1962 Frank Schmitz
1963 Wayne Miller, Univ. of Michigan.
1964 Wayne Miller, Univ. of Michigan
1965 Jim Yongue, Univ. of S.W. Louisiana
1966 Wayne Miller, Univ. of Michigan
1967 David Jacobs, Univ. of Michigan
1968 David Jacobs, Univ. of Michigan
1969 George Huntzicker, Univ. of Michigan
1970 Wayne Miller, Univ. of Southwestern Louisiana

AAU—Women

1961 Barbara Galleher, Dallas Athletic Club
1962 Beverly Avert, Univ. of Texas
1963 Judy Wills, Gulfport, Mississippi
1964 Judy Wills, Gulfport, Mississippi
1965 Beverly Averyt, Austin, Texas
1966 Judy Wills, Southern Illinois Univ.
1967 Judy Wills, Southern Illinois Univ.
1968 Judy Wills, Southern Illinois Univ.
1969 Vicki Bolinger, Springfield, Illinois
1970 Renée Ransom, Memphis, Tennessee

National AAU Synchronized Pairs
Men

1969 Jim Yongue and Don Waters, University of Southwestern Louisiana
1970 Gary Smith and Don Waters, Univ. of Southwestern Louisiana

Women

1969 Judy Johnson and Troy Kauffman, Centenary College
1970 Lucy Clauter and Diana Haney, Springfield, Illinois

USGF—Men

1963 Danny Millman, Univ. of California
1964 Gary Erwin, Univ. of Michigan
1965 Frank Schmitz, Southern Illinois Univ.
1966 Dale Hardt, Southern Illinois Univ.
1967 Dale Hardt, Southern Illinois Univ.
1968 Dale Hardt, Southern Illinois Univ.
1969 Stormy Eaton, Univ. of New Mexico
1970 Stormy Eaton, Univ. of New Mexico

USGF—Women

1963 Nancy Smith, Austin, Texas
1964 Judy Wills, Gulfport, Mississippi
1965 Judy Wills, Gulfport, Mississippi
1966 Judy Wills, Southern Illinois Univ.
1967 Judy Wills, Southern Illinois Univ.
1968 Judy Wills, Southern Illinois Univ.

NAIA

1964 John Tobler, Bemidji State
1965 Ray LaFrancis, Western Illinois
1966 John Tobler, Bemidji State
1967 Jim Yongue, Univ. of S.W. Louisiana
1968 Richard Wadsach, N.W. Louisiana State
1969 Steve Berger, Univ. of Wisconsin at La Crosse
1970 Steve Berger, Univ. of Wisconsin at La Crosse

Index